A WILLIAMSON W KIDS CAN!® BOOK

KIDS
Write!

Fantasy & Sci Fi, Mystery, Autobiography, Adventure & More!

by Rebecca Olien

Illustrated by Michael Kline

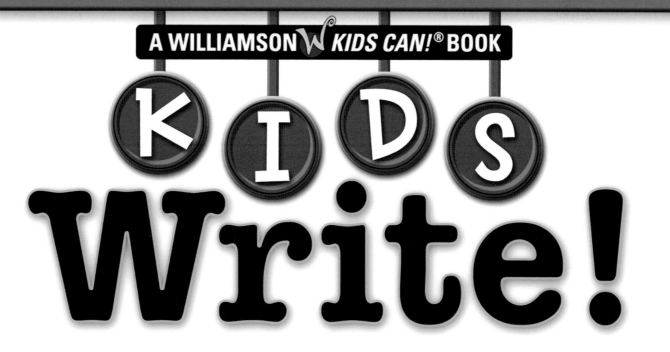

Williamson Books • Nashville, Tennessee

LIBRARY OF CONGRESS CATALOGING-IN-PUBLICATION DATA

Olien, Rebecca.
   Kids write! : fantasy & sci fi, mystery, autobiography, adventure & more! / Rebecca Olien ; illustrations by Michael Kline.
      p. cm.
   "A Williamson kids can! book."
   Includes index.
   ISBN 0-8249-6771-2 (pbk. : alk. paper) — ISBN 0-8249-6775-5 (hardcover : alk. paper)
   1. Language arts (Elementary) 2. Language arts (Middle school)
3. Creative writing (Elementary education) 4. Creative writing (Middle school) I. Kline, Michael P., ill. II. Title.
   LB1576.O435 2005
   372.62'3—dc22
                        2005014255

KIDS CAN!® SERIES EDITOR	Susan Williamson
PROJECT EDITOR	Vicky Congdon
INTERIOR DESIGN	Bonnie Atwater
INTERIOR ILLUSTRATIONS	Michael Kline
COVER DESIGN AND ILLUSTRATION	Michael Kline

Published by Williamson Books

An imprint of Ideals Publications

A division of Guideposts

800-586-2572

Printed and bound in Italy.

Dedication ● ● ● ● ● ● ● ● ● ●

To all my students who have made writing such a fantastic way to share and discover.

Kids Can!®, *Little Hands*®, *Quick Starts for Kids!*®, *Kaleidoscope Kids*®, and *Tales Alive!*® are registered trademarks of Ideals Publications, a division of Guideposts.

Good Times Books™, *Little Hands Story Corners*™, and *Quick Starts Tips!*™ are trademarks of Ideals Publications, a division of Guideposts.

NOTICE: The information contained in this book is true, complete, and accurate to the best of our knowledge. All recommendations and suggestions are made without any guarantees on the part of the author or Ideals Publications. The author and publisher disclaim all liability incurred in conjunction with the use of this information.

PERMISSIONS
Page 6: Permission is granted by the author to reproduce "How I Met My Robot Friend."

CONTENTS

4 Ready, Set, Write!

7 What an Adventure!

10 Treasure-Hunt Tale

14 Mini-Explorer Exploits

18 Superhero Saga

21 Adventure Flip Book

24 Drawn into Adventure

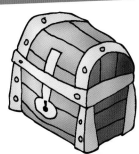

27 It's a Mystery!

31 Perplexing Triple Puzzler!

34 Spooky-Sounds Story

37 Haunted-House Hunt

40 Welcome to the Mystery Theater

44 Mystery in a Box

48 Top-Secret Mission
(Complete with Super Spy Gadget!)

52 Picture-"Purrfect" Pet Mystery

55 Amazing But True!

56 Famous Talking Head

60 You-Can-Do-It! Book

63 News Flash!

67 Folktales & Legends

68 Magical-Mask Fable

71 Tall, Taller, Tallest Tale!

75 Tale of the Trickster

78 How the Elephant Got Big Ears

81 Sci Fi, Fantasy & Fairy Tales

82 A Castle Chronicle

86 Space-Travel Tale

89 Robot Rescue Mission

92 Legend from an Imaginary Land

95 Magical Creature Myth

99 Meet Me & My Family!

100 Let Me Introduce Myself!

104 Our Fabulous Family! Magazine

107 Thanks for the Memories!

111 The Funny Pages

112 Make 'Em Laugh!

115 Crazy Comic Capers

118 World's Funniest Flip Book

121 Pass It On!

124 INDEX

READY, SET, WRITE!

Do you like to pretend, make up games, or create magical kingdoms and imaginary characters? When you let your imagination loose, you can come up with some really amazing people, places, and events. Would you like to capture those ideas and stories so that you — and others — can enjoy them over and over? That's easy — just write them down!

In this book, you'll go on adventures writing about superheroes, treasure hunters, and space travelers. You'll travel to make-believe lands full of magical creatures. You (and your friends) will laugh at jokes, cartoons, and silly stories you write for comic books. Spooky sounds, codes, and spy gadgets will add special effects to your mystery writing. You'll write about real people and events too, telling true stories about famous people you admire as well as those right in your family. Whether writing on a flip book, behind doors of a haunted house, or in your very own magazine, you'll discover interesting ways to use words — *your* words.

So, ready to have fun bringing to life the people, places, and events that make up unforgettable stories? Then sharpen your pencil and let's get started!

Rebecca Olien

Rebecca Olien

JUMP RIGHT IN!

You can begin anywhere you like in this book, depending on the kind of writing you're in the mood to do. Most activities call for a few simple supplies. Once you've gathered what you need, check out the **WRITER'S JUMP START**. This section gives you ideas to get your mind creating and the ideas flowing. Sometimes it's hard to begin with a blank sheet of paper! **READY TO WRITE** is a guide to start — and keep — your pencil moving. The questions in the writing steps will help you think of ways to develop your story. Remember, these ideas are just to get you started. You will often come up with your own way of writing your story.

What about editing?

Editing is the process of reviewing and changing your writing to make it better. When I write a story, I read it over several times, making changes here and there until it reads just the way I want it to. Try it — you may find you come up with a more interesting idea, a more exciting ending, or just a clearer way to say something. It always helps to have someone else read your writing to give you ideas, too.

The Never-Spell-A-Word-Wrong Dictionary

Jazz up your writing with exciting new words Thesaurus

THE WRITE STUFF

One of the best things about writing is that all you need is paper and something to write with. You can do it just about anywhere, anytime. It's fun, however, to jazz up your stories, especially when you write the final version. Here are some fun ideas!

- ◆ Showcase your story (or a collection of stories) in a handmade book. Use card stock or fabric-covered cardboard for the cover. Fasten the pages inside with staples, stitching, clips, ribbon, raffia, or colored wire.

- Type sections of your story and print on white paper. Glue them onto decorative paper for an attractive background (you'll find an amazing selection at craft or art supply stores). Include illustrations below the text if you like.

- Try cutting covers and pages into fun shapes. Put your purr-fect pet mystery (see pages 52 to 54) into a cat-shaped book or make a treasure chest–shaped book for your map adventure (see pages 10 to 13). How about a lightbulb-shaped book where you can jot down all your brilliant story ideas?

- Combine cutouts from old magazines to create intriguing collage-style illustrations.

- Decorate the pages with stickers, rubber stamps, stencils, or a decorative hole punch.

- Use colored pencils or watercolor paints for original illustrations.

This is a story about science and things people have found with microscopes.

This is a germ.

- Get creative with gel pens, glitter pens, and 3-D paint pens for the cover, title page, and important words throughout the story. How about glow-in-the-dark paint on black paper for the title page of your SPOOKY-SOUNDS STORY (page 34), for example?

How I Met My Robot Friend

I'm here to tell you a story about my best friend. He's not a person but he's still my best friend. He is a robot. My robot has a silver body. He can shoot razor blades and change size. He has two sets of arms: two on his shoulders and two on his sides. My robot's name is Beebie.

One day I was riding my bike home from school. I was almost home when I heard a beeping noise: Beep! Beep! Beep! Then I saw some silver. I looked through the bushes and saw a robot. "Hello, I am Robot SP 7943," said the robot.

Nick, age 8

WHAT AN ADVENTURE!

Calling all adventure seekers! Prepare to create untold tales of exciting exploits and fantastic feats!

Writing adventure stories lets you travel to exotic places, meet interesting characters, and tumble into (and out of!) all sorts of trouble. You might find yourself on a desert island following an ancient treasure map or flying over a field of sunflowers on the back of a bee! Let your imagination run wild.

Create a larger-than-life superhero or a teeny-tiny explorer. Whatever the size, you will have fun taking these characters on exciting adventures full of discoveries, surprises, and perhaps some danger! But don't worry. With each challenge, you will find an exciting way to save your character in the nick of time. Try out different ways to develop your terrific tales using flip books, super-sized figures, card games, and more.

So grab on to your imagination — and your pencil — and jump into action!

One of the keys to writing a good adventure story is to include lots of action. Here are some ideas to help keep your adventure stories full of events and excitement so they hold readers' interest from start to finish.

LOST ITEMS

When something important is lost, it adds suspense to the adventure. It could be the trail, a compass, a map, your pet, or the trip leader.

TROUBLE WITH SUPPLIES

Supplies are an important part of any adventure. When something goes wrong with them, you add conflict to your story. You might run out of water or food, or the boat overturns, the rope breaks, the jeep gets a flat tire, or the torch blows out.

BAD WEATHER

A storm, tornado, lightning, howling wind, blizzard, or desert heat adds danger to an adventure.

ENCOUNTERS WITH ANIMALS

Adventure stories often happen out in the wilderness. You might run into a bear, moose, cheetah, ostrich, shark, or fire ants. Animals might eat your food, claw up your tent, scare you, or protect you.

AN UNEXPECTED FIND

A shortcut, a cave, a tunnel, a map, a guide, a key, or other important object found at just the right time keeps the story moving forward.

PLOT: THE MASTER PLAN

So, you can think up lots of exciting events, but you aren't sure how to put them in order to create a good story. In writing, the chain of the events that leads the reader through the story is called the *plot*. Think of it as a master plan of what will happen from the beginning to the end. If you need help organizing the plot of your story, try following these steps:

1 **The Beginning:** Describe the scene. Introduce the main character, so readers can get to know him or her.

2 **Add Conflict:** Think of two different possible problems for your character — something to get the story moving. Leave both problems open to different outcomes. Add an unexpected challenge or even a little danger to keep your readers on edge.

3 **Now Add More Trouble:** Think of five ways your character could get into even deeper trouble or face more danger. Choose the most exciting one.

4 **Solve the Problem.** As a writer, you have many choices as to how your characters solve their problems. They might use luck, smart thinking, strength, creativity, or maybe they have help from others. Write three ways to get your character out of trouble and end the adventure. Which one fits this particular character and makes a dramatic conclusion to the story?

5 **What Changed?** Adventures often end right back at the same place they started, except something has been discovered along the way. Your character might learn she is braver, smarter, stronger, or more creative than she realized, for example. Or maybe a character learns something new about the land, animals, people, or history of a place he is exploring. How did your character change?

Treasure-Hunt Tale

What makes a better adventure than a hunt for treasure? Create a treasure map to guide your writing and your imagination, then let it inspire an exciting tale that follows the trail.

Map Legends

A map *legend* (also called a map *key*) helps people read a map. You can make a legend for your treasure map. Draw a small symbol on the map next to each important location. Draw a box on your map. Inside draw small matching symbols. Next to each symbol print the name of the location. Then when you use those names in the story, readers will know just where to find them.

forest

rock

swamp

cave

bridge

castle

WHAT YOU NEED

Scissors

Paper grocery bag

Crayons

Writing paper

Pencil

Writer's Jump Start

1 Cut open the paper bag so it lies flat. Make your map look old and well used by tearing the edges so they look ragged.

2 Decide on a treasure. It could be money or gold, or maybe it's the recipe for a secret potion that brings eternal life. Draw an X on your map where the treasure is hidden.

3 Draw six or more places on your map. The main character will have to travel to these places in search of the treasure, so to make an interesting story, make them unexpected and challenging places. They can be created by nature, such as swamps, forests, caves, and rivers. They can also include structures like castles, bridges, towers, and tunnels.

4 Draw a path that winds past and through all the places, ending at the treasure.

5 Add finishing touches by drawing in background scenes and adding color. When your map is the way you want it, crumple the paper into a ball, then flatten it smooth with your hands. Now your map looks age-old and mysterious, as if many treasure hunters have tried to figure out its secrets.

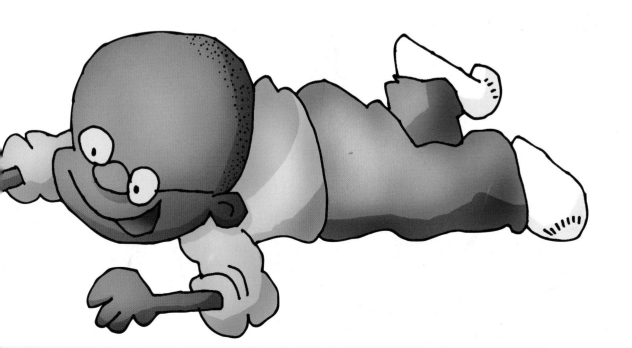

1 Make up names for the six places on your map by adding a descriptive word before each place like Stinky Swamp, Midnight Cave, or Creepy Castle. Number the places in the order they will be visited on the way to the treasure.

2 Begin your story by describing the main character — the treasure seeker. Write about why it is important for this character to get to the treasure. Does he want it for a good or a bad reason? Maybe he is poor, or the treasure was stolen from her, or the treasure needs to be found before it falls into the hands of someone dangerous.

3 Write about your character arriving at the first place on your map. Describe what the character sees, hears, and feels at this place. Is the place dangerous? Does the character need to solve a problem here before she can move on to the next place? Does she meet other characters here who help or *hinder* (hold back) her search?

READY 2 WRITE

4 Write about your character traveling to the next place on your map. Add danger or trouble for the character. How will your character need to think and act to continue on the treasure hunt?

5 Continue to write about your character traveling from place to place on your map. You might want to make things a little tougher as the character gets closer to the treasure. You can also have your character meet another character along the way. Will the new character help with or get in the way of the treasure quest?

6 Finish the story with the finding of the treasure. What does the treasure look like? How does the character feel when he or she finally finds it? Now that the treasure is found, what will the character do with it?

More Writer's Jump Starts

Pretend you are the main character. Picture this place in your imagination and describe it as you see it. See CHOOSING A VOICE, page 19.

Why Do I Start with a Map?

Aside from being fun to create, the map helps you work out how your adventure story is going to progress. After the character decides to seek the treasure, there are six steps that lead to finding it. The map is a fun visual way to develop the plot (see PLOT: THE MASTER PLAN, page 9) for this particular type of story. See pages 14 to 17, 24 to 26, 82 to 85, and 121 to 123 for some other creative ways to plan story plots.

Mini-Explorer Exploits

Have you ever thought about what a raisin might look like to an ant? It probably looks like a giant squishy wrinkled boulder. Create a story starring a tiny character where even something as small as a raisin becomes cause for adventure! The numbers in your story guide readers as they follow the string from stick to stick.

1 Draw and color a character on an index card. The character might be a person, an animal, or an imaginary creature.

2 Cut out the character and glue it to the craft stick, leaving some of the stick below the character. Give your character a name.

3 Choose a place for the adventure. It could be in your yard, at a playground, in your bedroom, or anywhere that looks like the scene of a wild adventure when you think small.

4 Play with your character in the setting you chose. Imagine what objects, sounds, and textures are like for your tiny character.

5 Write a number 1 on a craft stick and place it where you want to start your story. If outside, poke the stick in the ground. Inside, push the stick into a small blob of clay in a paper cup. You can stand your character up with a small bit of clay while you write.

6 Tie the loose end of the string to the numbered stick, keeping the rest of the string rolled in a ball.

Why Start with the Cups and String?

In addition to helping you develop the plot (page 9), setting up the cups and string before you start writing helps you to understand your character's point of view. Rather than sitting at your desk, trying to imagine what the world looks like to a tiny ant, you actually follow your mini-explorer's footsteps. Once you've experienced an ant's-eye view of the world, it's a whole lot easier to describe it to your readers. They'll have the fun of seeing it through the character's eyes, just as you did!

1 Write a big number 1 at the top of your story, and begin writing about the mini-explorer's adventure. Give your character a reason to explore. Maybe your character is searching for a rare animal, a lost treasure, another kingdom, a new route, or perhaps she is trying to prove something. Describe how your explorer arrived at stick number 1 and what it's like there.

2 Unwind the string as you pretend your mini-explorer is traveling to a new place. Wind the string around a second stick and place it in the ground or in a cup, as you did with the first stick. Label the stick with the number 2, and write a large number 2 in your story. Write about your character's journey to this second place. Have something adventurous happen at this new place. Maybe your character has to climb an extremely dangerous rock or stairway, ride in a soap bubble, fight through a spider web, find the way out of a leaf pile, or cross a scorching hot sidewalk.

3 Continue unrolling string and placing sticks at different stopping places. Keep labeling sticks and your story with numbers.

4 When you and your character have had enough adventure for one story, decide how the story should end. You can bring your character back to stick 1, or have your explorer decide to stay in a faraway place.

Remember, think small to create a BIG adventure. Your character might . . .

- ◆ meet a worm, insect, bird, lizard, or frog
- ◆ ride on a dandelion seed parachute, floating leaf, or twirling maple seed
- ◆ come to some sticky mud, quicksand, or a puddle
- ◆ meet your pet dog or cat
- ◆ find giant food like an apple, a peanut, or a banana
- ◆ have to get through a giant door
- ◆ take a ride on a skateboard

SUPERHERO ★ SAGA ★

Think of your favorite superheroes from comics, movies, and television. If you think they are fun to watch, they are even *more* fun to create!

My superheroine is **Tick Tock Tess**, who has the ability to stop time in order to help animals in distress.

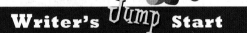

WHAT YOU NEED

Pencil

Large piece of butcher paper or cardboard

Tempera or poster paints

Paintbrush

Writing paper

Writer's Jump Start

Draw a large outline of a superhero on the paper or cardboard. You can draw it freehand or trace around a friend. Use paint to add details.

words for writers

CHOOSING A VOICE: FIRST, SECOND, OR THIRD PERSON

Did you name all your characters and use their names, or say "he" or "she," when you told what they were doing and saying? If so, you wrote in what's called the *third person*.

Try writing your superhero story in second person. *Second person* is when you use the word "you" instead of "I" or the character's name. You might say, "Whoa! Just when you think you're out of danger, your rear-view vision catches sight of an enemy tracking device on your trail." Writing in second person makes the reader feel as if he or she is the main character of the story.

What do you think it's called when you write using an "I" voice for the main character? You might say, "No problem. With my ability to pass through solid objects, I just stepped right through the wall of the nearest building and the tracker lost me." If you said *first person*, you're a good writer! First person is really fun because *you* get to have all the adventures!

1 Describe what your superhero looks like.

2 Write about your superhero's special powers. Is your hero extra smart, extra strong, or does she have other special powers?

3 How did your superhero get to be so super? Write about the first time your hero discovered she had special powers.

4 Uh-oh! Someone needs to be saved. How does your superhero use his or her extraordinary powers to come to the rescue?

ADVENTURE FLIP BOOK

1

Your rainforest report won you a trip down the Amazon! You arrive in Brazil by airplane and are escorted to your boat. You brought your best friend with you and the two of you are excited to start your jungle river adventure.

2

The river giude steers the boat out into the wide Amazon River. The air is heavy with the smell of fruit and flowers. Suddenly your friend cries out, "Ahh!" You turn around and...

Will you take the path through the jungle or go with the river guide? Writing a flip book lets you tell the same story with several different outcomes. Planning out your adventure first helps you develop the plot (page 9), exploring all the possibilities to create the best possible story.

WHAT YOU NEED

Construction paper, 12" x 18" (30 x 45 cm), 2

Scissors

Pencil

Ruled index cards, 3" x 5" (7.5 x 12.5 cm)

Computer (optional)

Glue

Crayons

Extras: stickers, magazine cutouts, scraps of colored paper

Writer's Jump Start

Make a Flip Book

1 Fold the paper as shown.

2 Open the paper up and you will see fold lines dividing the paper into eight rectangles. Cut down the middle and number the front and back as shown. Some numbers will be upside down. The section without a number will be the cover.

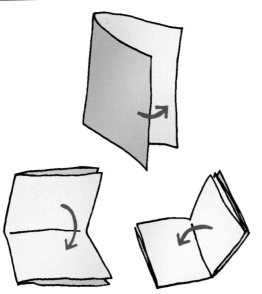

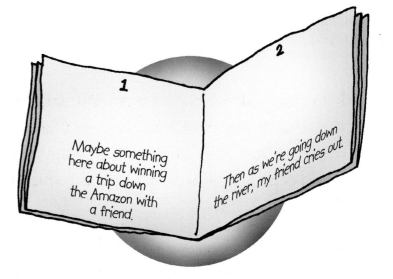

Maybe something here about winning a trip down the Amazon with a friend.

Then as we're going down the river, my friend cries out.

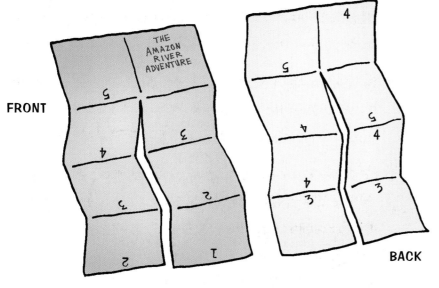

FRONT

THE AMAZON RIVER ADVENTURE

BACK

3 At the bottom of each panel, write out your ideas for your story, keeping in mind that it can develop in several different ways. In panel 1, write about how the adventure begins. Where are you? Start off with some action!

In the #2 panels, add conflict. Think of two different possible problems for your character. Add a little danger to keep your readers on edge. Leave each section open to different possible outcomes.

In the #3 panels, add even more trouble. See JUMP INTO ADVENTURE WRITING (page 8) if you need more ideas.

In the #4 panels, think up five different ways to get your character into even deeper trouble!

In the #5 panels, write three ways to get your character out of trouble and end the adventure.

1 Once you have a story that you like, write out each numbered section onto an index card, adding details as you write. If you need more space for your writing, type the sections in 5" (12.5 cm) columns, and cut them apart.

2 Glue each piece of writing into the section of the flip book so it covers up your story ideas as shown. Glue the writing right side up or upside down according to the numbers.

3 Decorate the pages, using cutouts, stickers, or drawings to illustrate your story. Make sure the numbers are still visible in each box. Write the title on the cover and decorate it.

4 Accordion-fold the book so the cover is on the outside. To read your book, begin with panel 1. Open and flip out pages to read your book in order through panel 5.

5 Fold the book closed again. Now try flipping the pages different ways (but still following from 1 to 5). You'll have to close some flaps as well as turn the book upside down to read all of the sections. You'll discover you've created many different adventures — all in one book!

Drawn into Adventure

Put some chance into your writing using a deck of cards that you create. Your characters will face a series of unrelated challenges, based on the cards you draw. *Your* challenge is to combine these events into an entertaining tale of adventure! (Don't worry, you'll draw some solutions, too!)

WHAT YOU NEED

Construction paper and markers or old magazines to cut up

Scissors

Glue

Index cards, 3" x 5" (7.5 x 12.5 cm), yellow, blue, and green

Writing paper

Pencil

Writer's Jump Start

1 Draw or cut out five or more pictures of characters you would like to imagine going on an adventure. Glue each picture on a yellow card. It is fun to draw or find different kinds of people. You might like some of your characters to be animals or objects. How about "The Adventure of the Runaway Sock," or "The Adventure of the Purple Octopus"?

2 Next, brainstorm (at right) a list of five or more places where adventures can happen. Draw or cut out pictures of these places and glue them on blue cards.

3 Finally, brainstorm a list of interesting objects that might be found or used on an adventure. Find or draw pictures to glue on the green index cards. To make your writing fun, include a few unusual objects such as a banana, vacuum cleaner, or squirt gun.

Yellow=Characters

Blue=Places

Green=Objects

words for writers

BRAINSTORMING

Brainstorming is a way of thinking up ideas. To **brainstorm**, you just write down everything that comes to your mind. Don't worry if your ideas are good or even whether they make any sense. Letting yourself write everything that enters your mind leads to more ideas. Later, you can go back and decide which ideas you want to use.

1 Sort your cards by color and place each pile facedown. Without looking, draw a card from the yellow pile. Begin writing your story by describing this character.

2 Draw a card from the blue pile. Write about your character doing something dangerous in the place on the card. Put your character in the middle of trouble (and leave him there!) before drawing the next card. This is called a *cliff-hanger*.

3 Draw a green card and write about your character using this object to help get past the danger. This part takes lots of creativity! Hmm … how can a banana help the explorer get past the herd of stampeding elephants?

4 Next, draw another card from the yellow pile. Write about the first character meeting this new character and how they continue on the adventure together.

Pick a card from the green pile. Have a character use this object to help save the character in trouble.

5 To complete your story, draw cards from any pile.

iT'S A MYSTERY!

Detectives, sleuths, and spies, grab your magnifying glasses and follow these clues to writing marvelous mysteries. Find out how to create suspense with creepy settings and shifty-eyed characters. Add startling discoveries, unexpected twists, and clever capers to keep your stories full of surprise. It's all part of writing a mystery!

To get started, you might decide to create a haunted house with surprises waiting to jump out from behind every creaking door. Or maybe you'll construct a super spy gadget complete with a transport module, rope thrower, mini-camera, recorder, lock picker, and other sneaky spy tools. The WRITER'S JUMP START sections show you how to design gadgets, sound makers, models, and puzzles to inspire your writing adventures.

You'll have even more fun when you include others. Write a mystery play, then gather friends to help you put on the show. There are even ideas for getting your pet in on the action. There's certainly no mystery about why these stories are fun to write!

JUMP INTO MYSTERY WRITING!

Having trouble thinking of a mysterious event for your story?
A mystery needs a problem for the main character to solve.
Here are some ideas.

SOMETHING UNUSUAL IS FOUND. IT COULD BE A ...

Key

Buried box

Bag of money

Mysterious photograph

Old map

Mysterious letter

SOMETHING IS MISSING. IT COULD BE A ...

Pet

Money

Homework

Candy or other food

Secret code to the location of something valuable

Toy

SOMEONE IS ACTING STRANGE. HE OR SHE COULD BE ...

Sneaking around

Telling secrets

Avoiding the main character

Hiding something

Running away

The main character needs clues to solve the mystery. Some clues are obvious — a witness (see MYSTERY-WRITER'S DICTIONARY, page 30) sees or hears something important or a character acts really suspicious.

Clues can also confuse the person trying to solve the crime. Maybe the criminal has deliberately left something for the detective to find that will throw her off the trail. Or maybe the detective interprets something as a clue, but it isn't. He might find some footprints that he thinks are the criminal's, for example, but they belong to someone else.

CLUES:
Helpful or Confusing?

Here are some different kinds of clues. Add your own clues as you think of them, or as you are inspired by ideas in other mystery stories or movies.

SOMETHING IS USED OR TAKEN ...

Key

Food

Phone book

Map

SOMETHING IS LEFT ON PURPOSE ...

Message

Ransom note

Riddle

Cassette tape

Videotape

SOMETHING LEFT BEHIND BY MISTAKE ...

Fingerprints

Tire tracks

Footprints

Phone number or address

Handkerchief with someone's initials

Hat, mitten, scarf, or glasses

Fur or feathers

MYSTERY-WRITER'S DICTIONARY

Mystery writers have a language all their own! Here is a list of words often used in mysteries to take the mystery out of their meanings.

accuse: to point out someone and say he or she did something wrong

alibi: proof someone accused of something uses to show he was not at the scene of the crime when it was committed

clue: something that gives information to help to solve a mystery

deduce: to figure out something about the crime from the clues and information

detective: someone who tries to solve a mystery

evidence: facts and objects that help prove something

investigate: to look for clues and information that help to solve the mystery

proof: facts that show something is true

red herring: a false clue that makes it seem as if something is important when it isn't and it actually leads away from the solution

scene of the crime: where the crime or mysterious event actually took place

solution: the answer to the mystery

suspect: someone who is thought to be guilty of the crime

suspicious: acting in a mysterious or guilty way

witness: someone who sees the crime

suspicious: acting in a mysterious or guilty way

PERPLEXING TRIPLE PUZZLER!

If you like puzzles, try this! First you write a mystery, which you turn into a type of puzzle where certain words are replaced with pictures, called a *rebus*. Then the whole story is turned into a jigsaw puzzle. Your final story has three different kinds of puzzles to solve!

One day [boy] was using his [scissors] to cut pictures from magazines for a school project. He found lots of [birds], but what he was really looking for was an [alien]! [boy] always dreamed of flying in a [space shuttle] someday and loved everything to do with [space]. "I would like some [gum]," he thought to himself, so he started for the store. But [boy] kept thinking about [birds], so he headed for the shed.

Writer's Jump Start

1 Choose an idea for your mystery. How about a story about an important item that is suddenly missing? Check out JUMP INTO MYSTERY WRITING on page 28 for some ideas.

2 Create some characters for your story — you'll need a main character (the person whose object is missing) and someone to search for it. The main character can search for his or her own object, or you can have fun creating a detective who solves the mystery. To make the story more interesting, add a few other people to help with or hinder the search.

3 Collect stickers of objects and characters that go with your story. You can also make your own stickers by drawing tiny pictures on the round label stickers. You'll make more stickers after you write your story.

WHAT YOU NEED

Picture stickers

Round label stickers,
    ¾" (2 cm) diameter

Markers

Writing paper

Pencil

Card stock,
    8½" x 11" (21 x 27.5 cm)

Scissors

Manila envelope,
    6" x 9" (15 x 22.5 cm)

1 To begin, write about the moment when your main character discovers that something is missing.

2 Describe how the detective tries to solve the mystery by finding clues. The detective might find footprints, a message, or a lost mitten. Most of the clues should lead the detective closer and closer to finding the object until the mystery is solved, but you might want to toss in a few red herrings (see MYSTERY-WRITER'S DICTIONARY, page 30).

3 Read over your story and decide which words you want to replace with pictures to create the rebus. Use the pictures you drew on the circle stickers, drawing more if you need to. Store-bought picture stickers work well for words that repeat often.

4 Copy your story onto the card stock. Every time you get to one of your chosen words, use a sticker instead.

5 Cut the story into 20 or more pieces. Vary the shapes to make the puzzle fun to put together.

6 Decorate the envelope and use it to store your puzzle.

It was a dark and stormy night, and ___ was watching ___. Outside the ___ would pop through every now and then. She decided to turn off the ___ and pick up her favorite ___ which was all about ___. Her ___ Roscoe started barking about something. ___ got up to see what was the matter, and took her ___ with her, and you'll never believe what she saw!

Spooky-Sounds Story

Eeerrrr-FOOP!

SCRaaaWK!

Beenk
Beenk
Beenk
Beenk

wub wub, wub wub,

What makes a scary scene in a movie that much scarier? The music and the sound effects! Write a spooky story, then use these sound makers to add rain, thunder, screechy screams, squeaky doors, and more when you tell it!

Sound makers: poster board; rice; metal cake or pie pan; paper towel tube; plastic shopping bag; blocks of wood, 2; cardboard box; string, 12" (30 cm); piece of fabric, 1" (2.5 cm) square

Writing paper

Pencil

Tape recorder and cassette (optional)

Writer's Jump Start

Explore different ways to make interesting and spooky sounds using the sound-maker materials.

- Hold the poster board by one corner and shake it so it sounds like thunder.

- Sprinkle rice in a cake or pie pan to sound like rain.

- Blow and hum through the cardboard tube to make howls or wind.

- Crumple the plastic bag to make sounds of walking through leaves.

- Tap the wooden blocks on a box for the sounds of footsteps.

- Pull a small piece of wet fabric along a length of string (pinching it tightly) to make sounds of screeches, screams, and squeaky doors.

1 Did you create some spooky sounds? Make a list of the ones you want to use in your story. Place a number next to each sound.

2 Begin writing your spooky story by describing a stormy night. Read your writing aloud. Where would a sound effect help readers to picture the setting or, better yet, to feel as if they were there? Note the sound-effect numbers in your story so you remember what sound to make and where.

3 Describe a character who is out in the storm. This character needs to find a dry place to go. How about a haunted house or an abandoned cottage? Describe the house. Add more sound effects of the storm. Is the storm getting worse?

SCRAAWK!

4 As you know, a good spooky story needs to get, well, scary! Write about your character going into the house. What sounds are in the haunted house? What else does the character see, hear, and smell as he or she goes from room to room? What's upstairs? Add sound-effect numbers for footsteps, creaking floors, or howls behind closed doors as you write. How does your character feel?

5 Now for the ending. What does your character find? It could be something really creepy. Or it's only some mice playing in the attic, knocking things over! You decide.

6 Friends or family can help you by making the sound effects as you read your story. After practicing a few times, perform the story for others or record it to play whenever you want to spook someone!

Haunted-House Hunt

Would you like to take your readers through a creepy place as they read your mystery? Here's how to "hide" your story in a haunted house full of mystery clues that readers follow as they hunt for a surprise character!

For other fun ways to lead readers through a story, see pages 21 to 23, 44 to 47, and 78 to 80.

Construction paper,
12" x 18" (30 x 45 cm),
4 pieces

Markers, colored pencils,
or crayons

Scissors

Ruler

Glue

Extras: fabric, cardboard
and paper scraps,
glow-in-the-dark marker

Writer's Jump Start

1 On one of the pieces of
paper, draw the outline of a
haunted house. Position the
paper so the house is wider
than it is tall. Color in broken
windows, doors with peeling
paint, overgrown bushes and
vines, broken boards, cob-
webs, and anything else to
make the house look spooky.

2 Turn the windows, doors,
and other secret places
on the house into flaps by
cutting around three sides
of each shape. (Be careful
not to cut around all four
sides or the window or
door will fall off!)

3 On another piece of paper,
draw a large triangle for
the roof as shown. Cut it
out. Trace this triangle onto
another piece of paper and
cut it out. Cut attic windows or secret doors in
one of the roof pieces.

4 Glue the roof triangle
with cutouts onto the
front of the house. Glue
the fourth piece of paper
and the other roof shape
to the back of the house.
Be careful not to put glue
on the backs of the door
and window flaps. When
you open the flaps, you
have blank spaces to
write on.

5 Fold the house down the
middle, then open it partway
so your house will stand by
itself.

6 Now, imagine a mischievous
creature hiding in the house.
It could be a spooky ghost
or skeleton, a silly monster,
or an animal such as a spider,
bat, or mouse. Where do
you want this creature to
be hiding?

18" (45 CM)

1 Write "Enter" on the front door. Open the door and write a clue to another hiding place in your house. Draw a picture to illustrate your clue.

2 Lead readers to the next clue by drawing a picture on the outside of the next flap you want them to go to. Be certain only one flap has that picture to make sure clues will be read in order.

3 Continue writing clues inside each flap to lead readers from secret to secret. Add drawings on the outside of windows, doors, and secret flaps to help readers follow each clue. Make the last clue lead to the secret character's hiding place.

I'm so glad you're here. Can you help me solve the problem of my haunted house? Maybe if you followed the dots...

WELCOME to the MYSTERY THEATER

Write a spooky script, then direct your own mystery play. Collect some friends for the cast, a few more for the audience, and then on with the show!

WHAT YOU NEED

Friends and family members (to act in your play)
Props (see page 43)
Writing paper
Pencil
Costumes

1 Determine how many friends and family members will be in your play so you know how many character parts to write.

2 Choose a stage area where actors have room to move around. It doesn't have to be fancy.

3 Collect props to use in your play. As you look for interesting objects and consider who will be in the play, you will begin to get ideas about the kind of mystery you want to write and the characters to create.

4 To help get your creative writing mind working even more, ask some of the cast to try out possible scenes with you. Some you will like, and some you may not. Use your best ideas to write the script (see page 43).

Ummm, not that kind of prop.

1 At the top of the script, make a character list. You might want to include a narrator who explains what is happening between scenes. Write the names of the actors and actresses next to their characters.

Detective Sam Snooper:
    This hat was found at the
    scene of the crime.
        (he waves the hat in her
        face)
    Is it yours?
Sally Suspect:
    No. I never wear hats. Besides,
    it's too small. See?
        (she tries to put the hat on
        her head)

2 Plays are written a little differently from stories. The dialogue (see page 43) doesn't use quotation marks, for example. The characters' actions are in parentheses.

3 A play needs a lot of action to hold the audience's interest, so be sure to keep the dialogue moving back and forth between characters and have them always doing something on stage. Check out JUMP INTO MYSTERY WRITING on page 28 when you need more ideas.

4 Make enough copies of the script for all the actors and actresses. Ask them to create simple costumes for their parts. A costume could simply be wearing a hat, tie, apron, or fake moustache.

5 Rehearse the play a few times. Make changes in the script to improve the story. Now you're ready for the final performance!

More
Writer's Jump Starts

Do you have a favorite mystery story? Turn the most exciting scene from the book into a short play. Write a script, then round up actors, props, and costumes.

PLAY-WRITER'S DICTIONARY

Here are some special words that are handy to know when you are writing and rehearsing a play.

act: a group of scenes. In Act I, for example, you could set up the mystery to be solved, and then in Act II, you could solve it.

dialogue: conversation between characters

playwright: person who writes the play (that's you!)

props: objects an actor or actress uses to help tell the story. A key, a flashlight, a book, a cane, or an umbrella are all examples of props.

scene: all the action that takes place in one location; when you change to a different location, that's a new scene.

script: the written copy of the play with all the dialogue and characters' actions and movement

MYSTERY IN A BOX

Create a mystery story that's stored in a special box. Open the lid to let the mystery unfold. Turn the story around and you have the background scene, so you can act out the mystery with tiny characters.

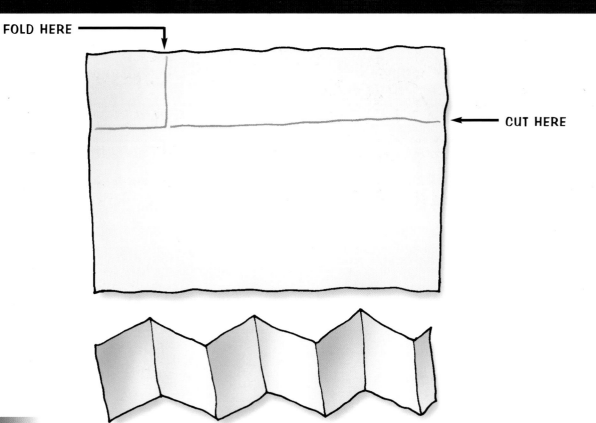

CUT HERE

WHAT YOU NEED

Pencil

Small cardboard box
(a jewelry gift box is perfect)

Drawing paper,
12" x 18" (30 x 45 cm)

Ruler

Scissors

Markers, crayons, or colored pencils

Index cards, unlined

Writer's Jump Start

1 Trace around the box onto the corner of the drawing paper. Use the ruler to extend the traced line as shown. Cut out the strip of paper along this line.

2 Fold the paper along the remaining line. Flip the paper over and accordion-fold it as shown until you reach the end. Cut off any extra paper that doesn't make a complete fold. Make sure the folded strip fits inside the box; trim one edge if necessary.

3 On one side of the strip, color a picture of the setting of your mystery. You can add more details after writing your story, but this drawing will help you picture the location and make it easier to imagine the events.

4 Cut pieces of index card to fit inside the box. On each one, draw a picture of a character you want to include in your story.

1 On the blank side of the paper, begin writing your story in the first section. Start off with some action! What does your main character discover? See JUMP INTO MYSTERY WRITING (page 28) for ideas if you need them. How does your character feel? Is he or she scared, startled, surprised, upset, angry, confused, or curious?

2 In the second section, write about why your character wants to solve the mystery. What kind of plan does your character have to solve it? Does your main character try and solve the mystery alone? Or does your character ask a friend to help? What is this new character like?

3 In the next section, write about a clue your character finds. Have the clue lead the character to do something that gets him either closer to or further away from solving the crime.

4 Continue writing about clues discovered to lead your sleuth closer to the solution. Add suspense by writing your character into some trouble. Maybe he almost gets caught looking for clues, or she gets locked inside a broom closet while spying on a suspect (see MYSTERY-WRITER'S DICTIONARY, page 30).

There we were, speeding along on our bicycles, trying to outrace the oncoming rain...

5 End the story on the last section. If you want to make a longer story, cut another strip the same size. Fold the second strip as shown in step 1 on page 45 and tape the strips together.

6 Turn the paper over and add more details to your setting illustration. Fold up the story, placing your cardboard characters in between the folds.

7 Print the title of your story on the outside of the box, and decorate the sides and cover.

More
Writer's Jump Starts

To make your story more puzzling, add a red herring (see MYSTERY-WRITER'S DICTIONARY, page 30) to lead the reader off track. For example, the muddy footprints that lead to the stolen bicycle turn out to be your dad's, not the thief's.

How Will Your Mystery "Unfold"?

Your little folded mystery story is a very handy device for figuring out, scene by scene, exactly how your mystery will develop and for helping you determine how your detective will solve it. For some other fun ways to develop a story's plot (see PLOT: THE MASTER PLAN, page 9), check out pages 10 to 13, 68 to 70, and 82 to 85.

Top-Secret Mission

(Complete with Super Spy Gadget!)

Spy stories are mysteries with a special character —the *spy* — who has an assignment that often involves uncovering secret information. Sometimes the spy has to break a code, for example. These stories usually aren't very realistic, and typically, the character uses gadgets that do amazing things to help her get information or get out of trouble. Equip your secret agent with a gadget so she can use it in your own action-packed spy story.

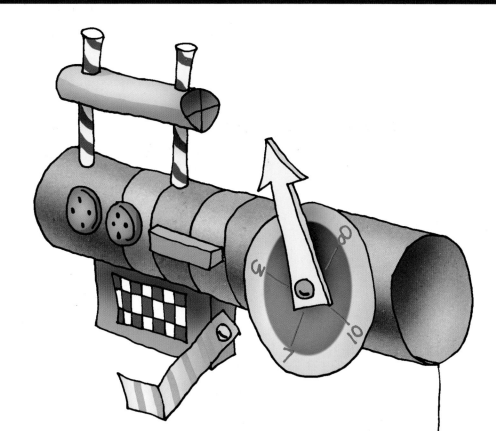

WHAT YOU NEED

Writing paper

Pencil

Construction paper

Crayons or markers

Gadget materials: small boxes, cardboard, string, paper towel tubes

Glue

Paper fasteners, buttons, bolts, and other small items for the controls

Writer's Jump Start

1 Imagine what you would like your spy gadget to do. Make a list of all its functions. Some ideas might include: decoding secret codes, sending messages, recording conversations, filming people, turning on and controlling the spy's car (handy for a quick getaway), detecting security systems, or shooting out rope for climbing.

2 Draw a picture to plan how you will make your spy gadget using the collected materials. You might find other things to use not listed.

3 Build the gadget by gluing parts together. Color or glue on buttons, switches, and other controls.

4 Play with your gadget as you write your story. It will help give you ideas for getting your character out of danger so she can complete the mission.

When Vicky opened her mail, she was surprised to find an unusual device with no note or anything. It was obvious that it was some kind of spy device. All she had to do was figure out how it worked. And the chance came the very next day when she was exploring an old warehouse. Suddenly, the lights went out and she was trapped. Then she remembered the device.

1 Begin writing about why the spy needs to get secret information. Why is the information important? How does the spy feel about the mission? How urgent is the mission? Will something bad happen to a lot of people — or maybe an entire city — if he or she doesn't complete the mission in a certain amount of time?

2 Write about the spy getting the gadget. Who gives it to her? Does the spy practice using it?

3 Write about the spy tracking down the information. Put the spy into danger. Maybe it is difficult getting inside a building. The spy might need to climb walls, or go through an underground tunnel. How does the gadget help?

4 Increase the suspense by making things more difficult and dangerous for the spy. How does the spy get past the trip wires, guards, video cameras, alarms, or guard dogs? Does anyone follow the spy? How does the spy find the key, break the code, or get into the safe without getting caught? How does the gadget help the spy?

Now write the spy story in first person (see CHOOSING A VOICE, page 19). Spy stories are especially fun to write in this voice because you are the main character, so you get to use the gadget!

5 Now add even more danger as the spy gets the information and escapes. Are doors closing, rooms being locked, people chasing him? Write your spy out of danger with the help of the spy gadget.

6 Write the ending with the mission accomplished and the spy ready to take on another secret adventure.

words for writers

SPY STORY— WRITER'S DICTIONARY

code name: the spy's secret name; for example, the famous secret agent James Bond's code name is 007 (double-oh-7)

decode: to figure out a message or instructions that are written in secret code

headquarters: where the spy reports to his or her boss to discuss the assignment

mission: the spy's assignment

secret agent: another word for a spy

undercover: using a different name and identity while on a secret mission

Picture-"Purrfect" Pet Mystery

WHAT YOU NEED

Camera
Pet
Heavyweight writing
    paper or card stock
Pencil
Glue

Do you wonder what your pet might say or do if it could talk? Here's a chance to write a story starring your pet as the mystery-solving detective! If you don't have a pet, use your favorite animal as the main character and illustrate the artwork with your own illustrations. Or, try using cartoon drawings (see CRAZY COMIC CAPERS, pages 115 to 117).

I knew that the tuna was in the locked cupboard, but a lock is a meaningless barrier to a cat of my skill. Soon the fishy delight would be mine...

1 Imagine your pet as a clever detective. What kind of mystery would it want to solve? What kind of clues could your pet sniff out? What troubles might your pet get into while solving the mystery?

2 Take a set of photographs of your pet doing its usual activities — eating, drinking, moving around. Try to get some close-up shots of different expressions or of your pet looking as if it's doing something that might lead to finding a clue (looking into a cupboard, peering under a bush in the backyard, or looking closely at something in the corner of its cage). You'll be using these photos in your story.

1 Begin writing about your pet discovering something is wrong. Maybe a favorite pet toy is missing or someone is eating its food, or it wants to solve a crime such as who stole your bicycle or who dug up the garden. Glue a photo showing your pet looking grumpy or confused.

2 Write about how your pet feels about this problem. Why does it decide to become a detective?

3 Write how your pet finds clues. Glue or insert pictures showing your pet doing different things like sniffing, looking up, or putting its head inside a paper bag or cupboard.

4 Continue to write about your pet finding clues. Make the story more interesting by having your pet get into some trouble while it's snooping around. Add photographs to fit with your writing.

5 End the story by having your pet solve the crime. In the final picture, your pet could be wearing a medal of honor or have a badge attached to its cage.

AMAZING BUT TRUE!

Think of all the things you know that are truly amazing — and true! Would you like to know more of them? How about ostriches taller than the tallest basketball player, a bald eagle's nest as big as a car, or an uncooked egg that can fall 700 feet (215.38 m) from a helicopter without breaking? Wow! And these facts are just for the birds!

Imagine the fascinating things waiting for you to discover about your favorite subjects. Learn about a famous person you've always admired or improve your skateboarding techniques or your maneuvers on the soccer field. There is no limit to the exploring you can do with a curious mind. Maybe you'll write in the voice of someone who lived long ago, or perhaps you're a modern reporter hot on the trail of a breaking news story.

Whatever projects and topics you choose, you are sure to be amazed by all the wonders in our world. So let's explore and share the topics that amaze you the most.

FAMOUS TALKING HEAD

Is there someone, from either the past or the present, whom you admire — an athlete, an actor or actress, or maybe a musician? Bring that person to life and let them tell his or her story with a "talking head"!

Before I wrote my first book, I wasn't famous at all. Now kids all over the world eagerly await more stories about a boy wizard who loves to play Quidditch. I'm sure you can guess who I am!

My name is Jackie Robinson, and 1947 was my rookie season for the Brooklyn Dodgers. I was the first black player in major league baseball.

In August of 1969, I stepped onto a place where no person had ever stood before. My name is Neil Armstrong, and I traveled to the moon and back!

Writing paper

Pencil

Balloon, 8" (20cm)

Old newspaper or plastic tablecloth

Old newspaper torn in 1" (2.5 cm) strips

Papier-mâché paste (at right)

Cardboard scraps

Tempera or poster paints

Paintbrush

Glue

Yarn

Extras: felt hat, scarf, costume earrings, baseball cap, etc.

Card stock or thin cardboard, cut into a strip 2" x 8½" (5 x 21 cm)

Stapler

Tape recorder and cassette

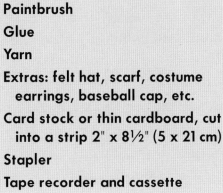

Making Papier-Mâché Paste

MATERIALS:

3 cups (750 ml) water; large bowl;

1½ cups (375 ml) flour; wire whisk

Pour the water into the bowl. Gradually add the flour, a little at a time, using the whisk to make a smooth paste.

Writer's Jump Start

Finding Out

1 Choose a famous person you admire. It could be an athlete, an actor or actress, someone from history, a political leader, a musician, an artist, or an author. Research this person's life using books, magazine or newspaper articles, and websites. Make notes of biographical information (where she was born, where she grew up, important accomplishments in her life, etc.) as well as other facts you find interesting.

2 Collect at least one photograph to look at while making the head.

Making the Talking Head

1 Blow up the balloon until it is head size. Tie it closed.

2 Cover your work area with newspaper or the plastic tablecloth. Dip the strips of newspaper in the papier-mâché paste. Hold a wet strip over the bowl and run your index finger and thumb down each side to take off extra paste. Wrap the wet strip around the balloon. Continue dipping strips this way, overlapping and crossing them until the balloon is completely covered. Let this first layer dry.

3 Look at the photograph of the person you are making. Use newspaper or cardboard scraps to create special features such as the nose, ears, chin, etc.

Add more dipped strips of paper to the rest of the head. Let this layer dry.

4 Add one or two more layers of papier-mâché; let dry between layers. Let the last layer dry *thoroughly* before painting.

5 Look at pictures of your person again before painting the head. Start by painting the whole head a skin tone color. Let dry, then paint the facial features.

6 Glue on yarn hair. Add a scarf, hat, costume jewelry, or anything else you like to complete the head.

7 Make a stand by stapling the card-stock strip into a circle. Add the person's name, just in case someone doesn't recognize him or her. Place the head on its stand as shown on page 59.

Use newspaper wads to make a nose, chin, eyebrows, and other features.

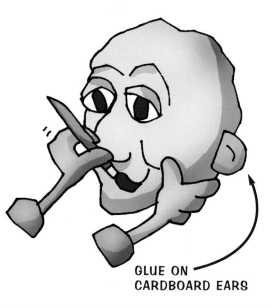

GLUE ON CARDBOARD EARS

1 Place your balloon head in front of you. Imagine what this famous person would have to say. Based on what you have learned about this person, how would he or she finish these thoughts?

My favorite things to do are …

The worst thing that happened to me was …

It's not always easy being famous because …

If you would like to follow in my footsteps …

I would most like to be remembered for …

2 Write a monologue (at right) for your famous person, using your list to help you decide what your person might say.

words for writers

MONOLOGUE

A speech or talk given by one person is called a *monologue.* In what person — first, second, or third — would you write a monologue for your talking head? Check CHOOSING A VOICE on page 19 to see if you are right!

The best thing about being famous is …

When I was your age …

Don't ever do this …

RINGO

3 Practice reading the monologue aloud. Experiment using different voices to make it sound more like that person and less like you. It's fun to add a little humor. Your character might ask if everyone is listening, sneeze, or tell a joke. (Warning: If you add too much humor, your audience will have trouble following the monologue.) When you feel ready, record yourself reading the monologue.

4 Set up the talking head with the tape recorder next to it. Add a sign that says "Push the play button." Stand back and watch as people listen to your talking head!

YOU-CAN-DO-IT! BOOK

Make a book that is full of fun activities for you and your friends (just like this one!). Teach others the skills and hobbies that you especially enjoy, and ask friends and family to contribute directions also, to create a book full of amazing things to do and make.

Skate Bored?
by Sara

Writing paper,
8½" x 11" (21 x 27.5 cm)

Drawing paper,
8½" x 11" (21 x 27.5 cm)

Construction paper or card stock

Writer's Jump Start

What do you like to do that you could teach others? What activities could other people you know write about? Choose the activities you would like to include in your how-to book.

A list of possible activities includes how to …

Make a spinning top

Take care of a goldfish, hamster, or other pet

Play Crazy Eights

Mix homemade play dough

Learn a few words or phrases in sign language

Teach a dog a trick

Draw a cat cartoon

Sew a hat

Fold an origami frog

Bake brownies

Do a skateboard trick

Conduct an experiment

Fly a kite

1 Write the title of the activity. Beneath the title, list the materials needed to complete the activity.

2 Write the directions step by step, numbering each step in order as you write it. It helps to do or make the activity as you write. That way you won't leave out an important step.

3 Include drawings to help illustrate tricky procedures and to show the completed project.

4 Repeat steps 1 through 3 to include as many activities as you like.

5 Make a cover from the card stock or construction paper and staple it in front of the activity pages. Or, for some other cover ideas, see THE WRITE STUFF, pages 5 to 6. Now your book is ready to be shared with others!

Graham Cracker
Doll House

MATERIALS:
1 BOX GRAHAM CRACKERS
1 CAN WHITE FROSTING
1 BAG OF Jelly beans

1) SKETCH A ROUGH LAYOUT OF WHAT YOU WANT YOUR DOLLHOUSE TO LOOK LIKE.

2) FIND A GOOD FLAT PLACE TO WORK

More
A Writer's Jump Starts

Does your uncle know a good way to cast a fishing line? Does your cousin draw awesome dinosaurs? Does your grandma bake the best-ever brownies? Maybe your neighbor grows beautiful sunflowers. Look around at what all kinds of people do. Ask as many people as you can to add a page for your book. Show them your activity as an example. Make enough copies so everyone who contributed to the book receives one.

NEWS FLASH!

Do you talk about interesting news stories and current events in school? Maybe you even have a favorite section of the newspaper that you like to check out. How about making a newspaper full of neighborhood news just for kids!

Extra!

The Neighborhood Gazette

Student Studies Slimy Slugs

When it was learned that local student Matthew Froomish was studying slugs, his mother nearly passed out. "Those things are gross!" she cried from the top of a kitchen step stool. Matthew was determined to continue his study of the slimy slugs however and set up an official slug laboratory in his room. His little sister had much the same reaction as his mom however and said that she would never set foot in his room again. "This is working better than I thought" exclaimed the young slug enthusiast. Thinking that he might find a cure for homework, Matthew continues his study.

Young Artist Draws On School Experience

The parents of little Bonnie Atwater were surprised to learn today that their daughter had been earning lunch money at school by drawing anime caricatures of her friends. "I think it's a good deal" she said.

1 Gather a team of friends to work on the paper. They can write articles, take photos, and help you decide what will go on each page. You'll need to choose a name for your paper and decide how many pages it will be and how many copies you'll need.

Will you type your newspaper and then insert the pictures on the computer? Or will you cut out the typed articles and glue them, along with the photographs, on pages to copy on a copier?

2 Discuss what you and your friends are interested in writing about. On this page you'll find some ideas for gathering community news. Make a list of articles for your first issue. Assign who will write each one.

Sports: What sporting events could you report on that involve kids you know? How about soccer games, ice skating, bowling leagues, horseback riding, and gymnastics? Try and scout out unusual sporting events for kids.

Places to Go: Articles about zoos, museums, parks, bike trails, nature centers, playgrounds, swimming pools.

Nature Spot: Nature news about local wildlife, plants, and weather. Also, how-to articles including fishing tips, camping skills, and outdoor safety.

Editorials: Letters giving a kid's opinion about a topic; most convincing when you use facts to back up your ideas and "make your case"

Comics: (See THE FUNNY PAGES, pages 111 to 123, for ideas.)

Pet of the Week: Ask your local Humane Society for a photo and description of one of the pets up for adoption.

Reviews: descriptions and opinions about books, movies, video or computer games, and toys

Classifieds: ads for things for sale or announcements of up coming events like family lemonade stands, garage sales, and fundraisers

1 Conduct interviews and collect information and facts for each article in your notebooks. A well-written news article should answer the five W's: who, what, where, when, and why.

2 Write the articles on the computer. Set the column width needed to fit three columns on each page (ask an adult for help, if necessary). Put the most interesting or most important information about the topic right at the beginning of each article to catch the reader's interest.

Name of paper

Big Headline Here

3 columns set up like these for the articles

A photo or artwork every now and then

Smaller headlines wherever they need to go

Writing Headlines

Reporters want to grab readers' attention right away. So they start with an eye-catching *headline,* or short title for the article. Headlines don't need to be full sentences. They often include alliteration or a play on words. *Alliteration* means using words beginning with the same letter or sound.

Scientist Studies Slug Slime

Baseball Becomes Big Hometown Hit

Earth Day is All-Around Fun

Kite Popularity Soars at Local Park

3 Take photographs and draw illustrations to go with the articles.

4 If you're creating your paper entirely on the computer, insert the photos and illustrations. An adult can help, if necessary. Otherwise, cut everything out. Rearrange the articles and photos in different ways on sheets of card stock until you have a look that will grab the reader on each page; glue them in place. Type the title of your paper in big letters and glue it in place across the top of the first page.

5 Make copies of your newspaper and deliver to your readers!

← NEWSHOUND

words for writers

NEWSPAPER-REPORTER'S DICTIONARY

assignment: the article or story a reporter is asked to write

banner: a big headline for a really important story

byline: the reporter's name either at the beginning or at the end of the article

edit: rewrite articles to be sure they are interesting and well written, and that all the facts are correct

features: main articles about interesting people and the most important events happening in your community

layout: the arrangement of the articles and the pictures on each page

lead: exciting start to an article that "hooks" the readers

proof: to read over the articles to catch any misspellings and other errors

FOLKTALES & LEGENDS

Imagine gathering around the campfire to listen to tales of the elders. Stories about why the beaver has a flat tail, why the rain falls, and how the Earth came to be fill your mind with images, as flames crackle and leap into the night sky. Every culture has its own favorite folktales and legends that are still told today!

But you don't need to live in the past (or even have a campfire) to create wonderful stories that explore our place in the world. Try your hand at creating legends starring clever creatures who outwit others with their wily tricks or larger-than-life humans who might lasso a cloud or use magical means to save the day. Invent a myth to explain a natural phenomenon, such as how the elephant got such big ears.

Sharing folktales is as fun as writing them when you act them out with a trickster character you create, make a moving story strip, or wear a magical mask. And don't forget to share your tales aloud in the age-old tradition!

Magical-Mask Fable ❧

Masks are like pretend faces. People all over the world enjoy making masks to use in storytelling.

Make a mask to help you write a tale of magic!

WHAT YOU NEED

Poster board or thin cardboard,
   12" x 18" (30 x 45 cm)
Pencil
Black tempera or poster paint
Paintbrush
Colored pastels or markers
Scissors
Glue
Extras: raffia, yarn, beads, feathers, ribbons
Wooden paint stick (from hardware store)
Writing paper

Writer's Jump Start

Make the Mask

1 On the cardboard, use a pencil to draw the shape of a large head with ears. Draw a face inside the shape, making the eyes, nose, and mouth big. Your face can look like a person, an animal, or an imaginary creature — just keep in mind that this is going to be a mask with special powers.

2 Paint over your pencil lines with black paint; let dry. Color your mask with pastels or markers.

3 Cut around the outer edge of your mask. Cut two small holes to peek through. (They don't have to be in the same place as your mask's eyes.) To make the nose stick out, cut around it as shown and bend it.

4 Glue on raffia or yarn hair, and other decorations of your choice. Glue the mask on the stick so you can hold it in front of your face as you tell your story.

5 Look at yourself in the mirror wearing your mask. Do you look silly, scary, or cute? Think about how wearing your mask makes you feel.

Why Do I Make the Mask First?

Wearing the magical mask is a lot like putting on a costume to be in a play. You can pretend to be someone or something you're not. In this case, the mask makes it easier to imagine that you have special powers. If you feel as if you're a magical character, it makes it easier to write from the point of view of one. The result? A more convincing story for your readers!

To try writing from another, very different point of view, see pages 14 to 17.

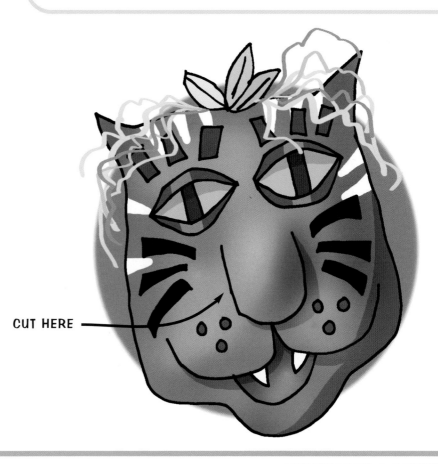

CUT HERE

1 Begin your story by describing how you got your mask. Did you find it or make it? Or was it given to you?

2 Now add some magic! Think of a special power your mask could have. It could make you invisible, strong, big, or small. What other magic could your mask have? Choose an idea and write a scene where you discover that your mask is magic. Describe how you feel when you put on the mask.

3 Now that you know the mask's magical powers, decide how your mask could help you. Write about a problem that needs solving. Maybe there is a lost dog in the neighborhood or a raging fire in a nearby forest, or your best friend's bike has been stolen. Write about how you put on your magical mask and come to the rescue!

TALL, TALLER, TALLEST TALE!

WHAT YOU NEED

Tall tales for inspiration (see MEET THESE LARGER-THAN-LIFE CHARACTERS!, page 72)
Writing paper
Pencil
Drawing paper
Colored pencils or crayons
Roll of adding-machine tape

Before television, people entertained each other by swapping tall tales after a hard day's work. These stories featured "super-sized" characters and their amazing exploits. The more unbelievable the character's adventures and exaggerated the tale, the better! Create a whopper of a tall tale — and see if anyone will believe it! If you like inventing adventures starring a larger-than-life hero, see pages 18 to 20.

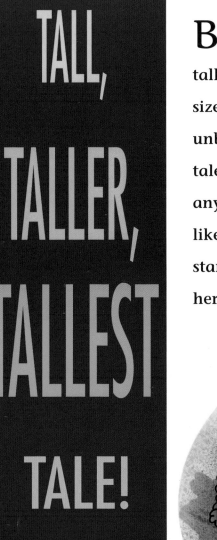

Writer's Jump Start

1. Read some tall tales to get the flavor of the exaggerated style.

2. Imagine a tall-tale character about your age. Think about which character traits would be fun to exaggerate — the character's size, strength, brain power, or speed are just a few examples. Jot down your ideas and decide which ones to include in your story.

3. Draw several scenes from your life at school and at home. Include things like having dinner, playing at recess, having a music lesson, studying math, painting in art class, helping with chores at home, riding your bike, and other everyday activities.

4. Now, imagine that same scene, only with the tall-tale character joining you. How does this change what might happen at each event?

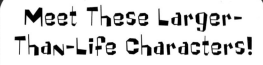

Meet These Larger-Than-Life Characters!

John Henry: An American Legend
by Ezra Jack Keats

Paul Bunyan,
Pecos Bill,
and
Sally Ann Thunder Ann
Whirlwind Crockett
(all three)
by Steven Kellogg

American Tall Tales
by Mary Pope Osborne

READY **2** WRITE

1 Write your story on the adding-machine tape, unrolling the tape into a "taller" and "taller" story as you go. Remember, a tall tale is written as if it is believable, no matter how ridiculous the story becomes.

Begin by describing your tall-tale character. To help add exaggeration to your descriptions, use similes (see page 74). Or, instead of saying, "Jim was tall and thin, and he had big feet," you might say, "Jim was taller than the flagpole on the school playground, and his feet were the size of skis." Your readers won't have any trouble picturing that!

2 Explain what funny and amazing things your character can do because of his or her special traits. For example, "With his big feet, Jim could hop faster than a kangaroo and higher than the Empire State Building."

3 Choose one or more of your drawings and write your tall tale describing what happens when your character joins in the event. Describe how your character creates some problems but also solves other problems because of his or her exaggerated traits.

4 Cut the story strip off the roll and hang it up in a place where others can enjoy reading your really tall tale.

But when Franklin got to the play-ground, he realized he had forgotten to bring a long stick to pry his basketball from the tree. Luckily, Long Tall Leon was with him, So Leon simply picked the basket-ball from the tree bending down (Leon was THAT tall!). Now everyone could play!

SIMILES

A *simile* compares two things using the words "like" or "as." Similes work especially well in tall tales, poetry, and other kinds of writing where you want to create especially strong images in the reader's mind. Which sentences you do find more descriptive?

The fly buzzed.

The fly buzzed like a helicopter.

He smiled.

His grin was as wide and toothy as a crocodile's.

Tale of the Trickster

Tricksters are animals or humans who outwit others with their cunning and tricks. These characters appear in folktales around the world. Here are a few characters that you may already know or could look for stories about: Baba Yaga (Russian); Anansi Spider (West African); Brer Rabbit (African-American); Coyote (Native American); the Monkey King (Chinese); and A-Chey (Cambodian). Sculpt your own trickster character and then write a tale or two about its crafty tricks.

WHAT YOU NEED

Paper bags in a variety of sizes

Newspaper

Masking tape

Glue

Cardboard scraps

Tempera or poster paints

Paintbrush

Extras: small boxes, feathers, glitter, sequins, foil, pipe cleaners, yarn, old clothing

Writing paper

Pencil

Writer's Jump Start

1 Choose the kind of trickster you wish to create. Many folktale tricksters are animals, but they can be human characters too.

2 To make the head and body, fill two bags with crumpled newspaper and tape them closed. Glue the bags together, holding them together with masking tape until the glue dries. Attach other features such as ears, horns, spikes, and a tail cut out of cardboard.

3 Paint the trickster. When dry, add finishing touches such as yarn hair, an oatmeal-box hat, feathers or sequin scales, old clothing, or pipe-cleaner whiskers.

4 Use your imagination to have some conversations with your character, so you can get to know its strengths and faults.

WRAP BALLS OF NEWSPAPER IN MASKING TAPE TO FORM A LONG NOSE OR SNOUT

GLUE OR TAPE ON NEWSPAPER TUBES AS LEGS AND ARMS

1 Introduce your trickster by describing where this character lives.

So readers get to know your tricky character, write about what it likes to do most of all. Maybe it has a favorite food that it searches greedily for or there is a special song that soothes it. Or maybe it loves to tell jokes or only talks in riddles. What other character traits does it have? Is it vain and does it think a lot about looking beautiful? Or is it always trying to teach someone a lesson? Maybe it's really bossy and wants to be in charge all the time!

2 Introduce one or two other characters the trickster needs to fool in order to get what he or she wants. What are they like? Does it seem as if they will fall for the trickster's tricks?

3 Unfold the trickster's plan as you continue to write the story. What kind of trick is played?

4 Does the trickster's plan work? Or does the other character outwit the trickster? You decide!

HOW THE ELEPHANT GOT BIG EARS

Many cultures all over the world hand down *myths,* stories that explain the workings of the world. In the past, these stories helped explain things, such as natural events, that people didn't understand. Today, we use science to explain many things that were once a mystery. Yet even with science, we still enjoy clever stories about why things are the way they are. Choose something interesting about a favorite animal and write a colorful tale that explains why it's that way.

It's a long story.

I have lots of time.

4" (10 CM) APART

2½" (6 CM)

WHAT YOU NEED

Pencil

Card stock,
8½" x 11" (21 x 27.5 cm)

Markers

Scissors

Ruler

Roll of adding-machine
tape, 2" (5 cm) wide

Writer's Jump Start

1 Draw a favorite animal on the card stock. Make the animal big enough to fill the paper.

2 Color the animal with markers and cut it out. Cut two slits as shown.

3 Make a list of traits your animal has that make it unique from other animals. An elephant, for example, has baggy skin, a big body, a trunk, tusks, and big ears.

4 Think of how the animal might look without one of these traits. For instance, imagine an elephant with tiny ears. Draw a picture if that helps you to visualize it.

Everywhere that Mohi went, she would bring food to some of the smaller animals, especially the mice.

Mohi was always kind to all the animals of the forest, even the tigers and panthers,

But one day when Mohi was walking through the forest, she noticed that the birds had suddenly stopped singing.

...began to hear ...that she ...recognize ...when she ... treetops,...

1 Begin by writing about the animal without its trait. What is its life like? What difficulties does it have?

2 Think of two or three events that could cause the animal to change to look the way it does today. Write your story on the adding-machine tape so that the story is written in one long line.

3 Thread the paper through the slits in your animal cutout. To read the story in the window, pull the paper along.

More
Writer's Jump Starts

How about a Collection of Myths?

Write a few more (or many!) myths and collect them in a handmade book (see THE WRITE STUFF, pages 5 to 6.) Here are some ideas:

How the Tiger Got Its Stripes
Why Leaves Turn Colors in Fall
Why the Eagle Has a White Head
Why Thunderclouds Are Dark
Why the Moon Waxes and Wanes

SCi Fi, FANTASY & FAIRY TALES

Turn your pencil into a magic wand to write stories about enchanted creatures, lofty castles, and fantastical faraway lands. Create wise wizards, winged fairies, futuristic robots or fearless space travelers as characters for your stories. Take them on other-world adventures, give them magical powers, and SHAZAM!, you've created a fantasy!

Maybe you'd like to tell a fairy tale from a different point of view. If so, there might be a fire-breathing dragon, hideous troll, or a shy fairy just waiting for you to bring it to life so it can set off on a magical adventure. Perhaps you will want to be like Dorothy in *The Wizard of Oz* and travel to an amazing imaginary land. All you need to design your own magical landscape is a batch of salt dough. If distant planets and intergalactic worlds is where your imagination takes you, than build a rocket and a tiny astronaut so you can blast off into outer space. You'll discover that not even the sky is the limit when you are writing these fantastical tales!

A Castle Chronicle

Make a castle with towers, turrets, banners, trapdoors, a throne, a treasure room, and more! Now you have the perfect setting to create a fanciful story with knights, princesses, a wizard, and maybe a dragon or two. These stories are so much fun to write, you might want to create a whole book about what goes on in this castle (see THE WRITE STUFF, pages 5 to 6).

WHAT YOU NEED

Cardboard

Cardboard tubes from
   paper towels or
   wrapping paper

Small boxes with covers

Scissors

Tape

Glue

Crayons, colored pencils,
   or markers

Colored construction paper

Tempera or poster paints

Paintbrush

Toothpicks

String

Small toy figures (optional)

Writing paper

Pencil

1 Use a large sheet of sturdy cardboard for the base of your castle. Use cardboard tubes for towers and pieces of cardboard for walls. Arrange small boxes inside the walls for special castle rooms and chambers. Color details inside each box and use cardboard scraps and construction paper to make furniture, a throne, and other props.

2 Paint your castle to look as if it's made of stone. Paint pathways, a courtyard, gardens, a moat around the outside, or anything else you'd like.

3 Cut out a cardboard castle door. Poke a piece of toothpick into the bottom of each side of the door. Poke the other ends into the door frame of the castle. Fasten string to the top to pull it open and closed.

4 Make cardboard people and animals for your castle or use small toy figures.

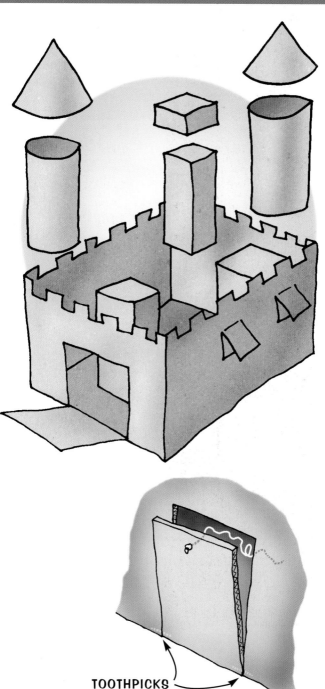

USE SMALL
BOXES FOR
ROOMS

CUT DOORS
FOR SECRET
PASSAGEWAYS

NOTCHED
CARDBOARD
FOR WALLS

TOOTHPICKS ←

Why Do I Start with a Castle?

What better way to imagine exciting scenes involving trapdoors, secret passageways, and everything from a fire-breathing dragon locked in a dungeon to a princess in distress in the topmost tower than to have a mini-castle where you can act them out? The castle is a fun, creative way to develop your story's plot (see page 9). If you'd like to try using a treasure map to work out your story's plot, see pages 10 to 13. Does playing a card game to determine your story events sound like fun? See pages 24 to 27.

1 Choose a main character. Is it a knight, princess, king, queen, wizard, sorceress, or dragon? Name your character and think of a reason why he or she might want to go to the castle. Is it to seek a fortune, to meet another character, to ask for help, or to pursue a quest? Begin your story by describing your character and his or her reason for traveling to the castle. See THE POWER OF THREE, **page 97.**

2 Describe your character's journey. Does your character have trouble along the way or meet anyone? Write about how your character feels when he or she finally arrives at the castle door? What does your character see and hear?

3 Is it difficult for your character to get inside the castle? Explain how your character enters the castle — what is the first thing that happpens? Write about what and who your character meets.

4 Where will your character go? Include the different places you created in your castle in your story. Is there something your character finds hidden? Does your character need to hide from anyone? Add excitement and a little danger. Write about your character getting into deeper trouble. Maybe your character is captured.

5 Who is going to help? Will magic be used? See MAGICAL NOTIONS, at right, for some ideas. Finish your story with a dramatic rescue, if necessary. Was your main character able to accomplish his or her original goal?

Magical Notions

Fantasy stories and fairy tales rely on magic to both add trouble and find solutions. Aside from wands and potions, here are some other magical items to use in your stories: crystal, ring, coin, pebble, hat, powder, mirror, apple, box, necklace, door, tree, cloak, sword, staff, shield, crown, parchment, feather, and unicorn horn.

Magical creatures include: unicorns, trolls, elves, dwarfs, fairies, centaurs, goblins, ogres, giants, and phoenixes.

Here are some things magic can do: make someone invisible; grant wishes; give special powers; turn something into something else; see into the future or past; change a character's size or appearance; make something or someone appear or disappear. You can probably think of lots more!

More Writer's Jump Starts

Have you always want to have the starring role in a fairy tale? Use first person (see CHOOSING A VOICE, page 19) to write your story!

SPACE-TRAVEL TALE

To create a tale of outer-space travel, all you'll need is a mini-space traveler and a spaceship. Then you're ready to imagine adventures on other planets and who knows, even in other galaxies!

WHAT YOU NEED

Plain clothespin (nonpinch type)

Markers

Foil

Pipe cleaner

Clear top from spray bottle

Glue

Construction paper

Potato chip can

Cardboard

Scissors

Tape

Balloon

Writing paper

Pencil

Writer's Jump Start

Make an Astronaut
On the round top of the clothespin, use the markers to draw a face and hair. Wrap the clothespin in a foil spacesuit.

Make a Spaceship
Glue construction paper around an empty potato chip can. Decorate the rocket with markers.

Make an Alien
Blow up the balloon and tie it closed. Draw a face and other features with markers.

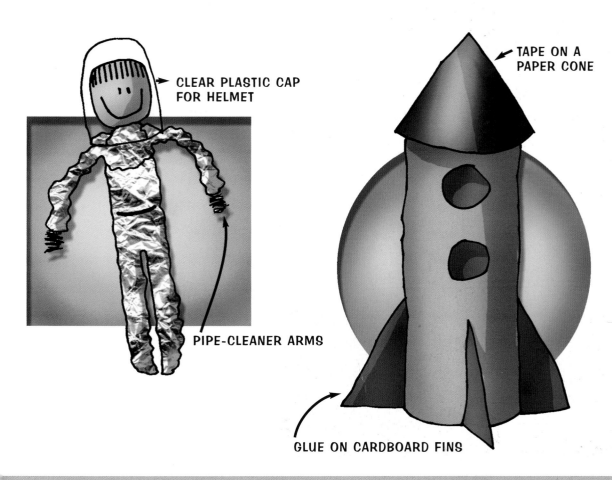

CLEAR PLASTIC CAP FOR HELMET

PIPE-CLEANER ARMS

TAPE ON A PAPER CONE

GLUE ON CARDBOARD FINS

TAPE ON CARDBOARD FEATURES

More Writer's Jump Starts

Have you always wanted to travel to outer space? Write your story in the first person (see page 19) so that you can be the astronaut and have the intergalactic adventures!

1 What does your astronaut have to do to prepare for space travel? Put your astronaut inside the rocket.

2 Lift off and take your rocket for a ride through space. Where will the rocket land? It could travel to new worlds in the garden, bedroom, basement, or cupboard. It could visit an imaginary land (see LEGEND FROM AN IMAGINARY LAND, **page 92**). A blanket can be a landscape of hills, valleys, and underground tunnels. A staircase becomes a steep mountain. Let your imagination take you and your astronaut on an other-world adventure. Write about what the astronaut experiences on this new planet.

3 Place the alien in this new world. What happens when the astronaut meets the alien? Use the alien's balloon body to add some fun to the encounter. The alien might …

★ Take the astronaut for a bouncing ride.

★ Stick to places with static electricity. (Rub the balloon on your hair and it will stick to the wall or ceiling, if it's not too heavy.)

★ Launch the rocket by letting out some air.

★ Attack the astronaut — who may have to resort to popping it!

★ Deflate in order to fit inside the rocket and return home with the astronaut.

4 Finish your story by getting your astronaut safely back home again, ready for the next adventure.

ROBOT RESCUE MISSION

Create a robot to be your companion on adventures that take place in a futuristic world. Give your robot some special powers so it can perform a dramatic rescue! If you enjoy creating stories starring a powerful character who can do amazing things, see SUPERHERO SAGA on pages 18 to 20.

Duct tape

Cardboard boxes, various shapes and sizes

Shoeboxes, 2 (same size)

Silver-colored dryer exhaust tubing, two 24" (60 cm) pieces

Tempera or poster paints in silver, black, and red

Paintbrush

Glue

Extras: colored coated wire, stick-on reflectors, stickers, nuts, bolts, bottle caps

Writing paper

Pencil

Writer's Jump Start

1 Use the duct tape, boxes, and tubing to create your robot. Paint it silver; let dry.

2 Paint on a face. Also, paint or glue on objects for the robot's controls of buttons, knobs, wires, and dials. Add any other finishing touches.

SMALL BOX FOR HEAD

DRYER TUBING FOR ARMS

SHOEBOX FEET

1 Begin the story writing about the creation of the robot. Who made it? How did it come to be yours?

2 Describe what the world is like in the future. What sorts of cool gadgets do people use? What do you and your robot do together? How do you spend your time?

3 Think of a problem your robot could help solve. Maybe you are kidnapped by another robot and he has to get you back. Or perhaps she has to help defend the planet against an attack of aliens.

4 Tell the story of how your robot comes to the rescue. Do her buttons and dials give her special powers? How does he use them?

words for writers

VERBS = ACTION WORDS

Verbs (words that describe what your characters do) are **action words**. Some verbs show more action than others. Fly, walk, hold, and ride indicate a little bit of action. Soar, scurry, grip, and gallop, on the other hand, give the reader a much clearer picture of exactly how the character is moving. Look for ho-hum verbs in your writing and replace them with more exciting verbs to pack your story with exciting action that the reader can easily visualize.

—LEGEND FROM—
An Imaginary Land

Create the landscape of a magical place from your imagination. Now you have the perfect setting in which to invent all kinds of fantastical tales!

WHAT YOU NEED

Heavy corrugated cardboard or Masonite board, 18" x 18" (45 x 45 cm)

Pencil

Salt dough (see page 93)

Spatula

Food coloring, green and blue

Plastic spoon, fork, and knife

Toothpicks

File folder label stickers

Tempera or poster paints

Paintbrush

Scissors

Index cards, unlined

Markers

Modeling clay, variety of colors

Writing paper

1. To begin imagining your magical land, pretend you are looking down on it from an airplane. Draw an outline of its shape on the cardboard or wood base.

2. Mix a batch of salt dough. Use the spatula to spread the dough in a layer over the shape drawn on the base.

3. Mix another batch of salt dough, this time adding a few drops of green food coloring to the water. Use this dough where you want hills, ridges, and mountains. Use the plastic silverware as tools to smooth or add texture to the landscape. Be sure to add places where characters could have adventures, such as caves, rocky cliffs, or a secret tunnel through a mountain.

4. Mix a third batch of dough, adding a few drops of blue food coloring to the water. Spread the blue dough on the landscape to form lakes, rivers, and waterfalls. How about a swamp where a character might get stuck?

5. Poke toothpicks into the dough at special places you would like to name. Print place names on labels and stick on toothpick posts. For example, you might want to name caves, rivers, waterfalls, lakes, and forests.

6. Wait several days until your magic land is completely dry. Paint on additional colors; let dry.

7. Cut figures and buildings from index cards and color them in. Remember, this is a magical place, so things might look much different from those on Earth. Use small bits of clay to stand them in place. Make other objects such as trees or 3-D creatures from clay.

8. Play with the characters in the magical land to imagine scenes and situations for your story.

Salt Dough

Measure into a bowl: 1 cup salt (250 ml); 2 cups flour (500 ml); 2 tablespoons vegetable oil (25 ml). Stir in 1 cup water (250 ml), a little at a time, until mixture is smooth.

1 Choose one of the characters you made from index cards or clay to be the main character of your story. Describe the magical place where this character lives. Write about what he or she does in this magical land.

2 Write about a problem the character discovers. Maybe the magical land is being threatened by a fierce dragon, a treasure is stolen, or a plot against the land's ruler is discovered.

3 Take the character on a journey through your magical land to solve the problem. Write about each place the character goes and what happens there. Use THE POWER OF THREE, page 97, in your story, if you like. Does the character use magic to resolve things? If so, see MAGICAL NOTIONS, page 85.

If you like creating adventures in your imaginary land ...

... you'll love making them up in your very own castle (page 82). These are both creative ways to get your imagination working, which gets the story ideas flowing. And you can actually try out situations and events for your story's plot (page 9). For some other fun ways to explore plot and character development, see pages 14 to 17, 18 to 20, and 75 to 77.

Magical Creature Myth

Mermaids, giants, unicorns, fairies, dragons, wizards, nymphs, gnomes, trolls, and ogres, oh my! Imaginary and mythical beings put the "fairy" into fairy tales and add the "fantastic" to any fantasy. Make up your own character to travel through a magical adventure in your imagination.

HEY!

Drawing paper

Colored pencils

Oven-bake clay, variety of colors (for use with adult help)

Extras: feathers, felt scraps, toothpicks, glitter, sequins, yarn, pipe cleaners

Writing paper

Pencil

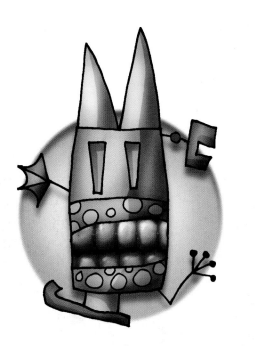

Writer's Jump Start

1 Imagine a creature for a fairy tale. It might have some of the characteristics of creatures you especially like from favorite movies or stories, but also try adding new features to create something original. Here are some to consider: wings, a snout, fangs, claws, feathers, spikes, scales, fur, fins, horns, and a tail.

2 Sketch several pictures of the creature until you create one you'd like to use in a story. Form the character out of the clay. Ask an adult to bake the figure according to package directions. Let cool.

3 Embellish your creature with accessories such as a magic wand, hat, feather boa, glitter, or anything else you like.

1 Make a list of words that describe your creature's personality (see page 98). Keep these in mind as you write your story and develop your character. Fairy tales traditionally begin with "Once upon a time …" but you can begin another way, if you like. Introduce your creature by describing where it lives and what it looks like.

2 Give your character a goal. What does your character want most of all? The goal helps readers understand the creature's personality traits. It also gives your story a focus. In your story, the creature will have adventures trying to reach this goal (see THE POWER OF THREE, at right).

3 Add stumbling blocks and problems. What other characters are in the story? Do they help or get in the way of your character reaching the goal? (If you get stuck writing a scene, try making these characters from clay as well and acting out some different ideas.)

4 Does your character succeed? Write the ending of your story. Does your story end with "They all lived happily ever after"? Most fairy tales do!

The Power of Three

Three is a common number in fairy tales. Sometimes a character is granted three wishes. Other times there are three problems the character has to solve or three tasks to complete, each one a little trickier than the last. The final wish or problem is always the most surprising, dangerous, or difficult. Try using the magic number of three in your story.

words for writers

MAGICAL CREATURE CHARACTERISTICS

How many of these traits does your imaginary creature possess?

angry	friendly	kind
bossy	fussy	nervous
brave	generous	picky
calm	greedy	reckless
careful	grumpy	shy
dishonest	helpful	silly
excitable	honest	strong
fearless	joyful	weak

More Writer's Jump Starts

It can be fun (and interesting for your readers) to make a character act differently from the way it looks. For instance, your very fierce-looking dragon or monster could turn out to be gentle and kind, while a cute, cuddly little creature might have a nasty temper. Surprise your readers with a character that doesn't act the way they might expect!

MEET ME & MY FAMILY!

Some of the best stories in the world are those handed down right in your own family — think of them as personal folktales! Travel adventures, encounters with nature, and humorous escapades are all more interesting when they involve the people you care about the most. I love to hear stories about my father's stormy fishing trips or my mother's friendly encounter with a gigantic snake. Here are some entertaining ways to write the stories in *your* life.

Writing personal stories is even more fun when you turn them into homemade books and or present them in other creative ways. Try making a life-story time line or a family magazine! Whatever you choose, you'll find writing is contagious when it is a family affair. Don't be surprised if you get more help then you bargained for!

Let Me Introduce Myself!

These stories are all about one fascinating topic — you! Use your first-person voice (see page 19) loud and clear to share those big "first times" and other important memories in your life. Continue to add to this book as new events happen in your life!

Roll of adding-machine tape

Pencil

Ruler

Family photo albums and baby books

Scrap paper

Writing paper

Blank book, purchased or handmade (see THE WRITE STUFF, pages 5 to 6)

Extras: colored pencils or crayons, drawing paper, photos

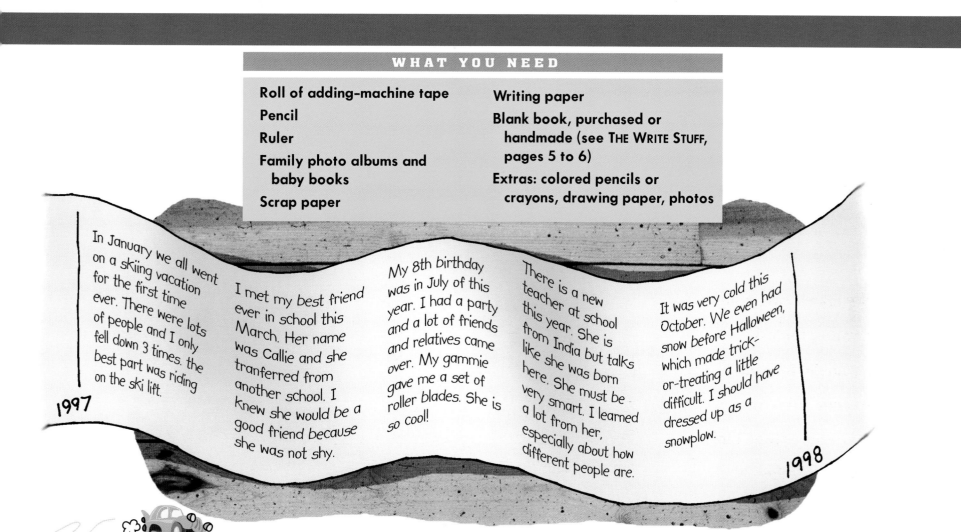

1997

In January we all went on a skiing vacation for the first time ever. There were lots of people and I only fell down 3 times. the best part was riding on the ski lift.

I met my best friend ever in school this March. Her name was Callie and she tranferred from another school. I knew she would be a good friend because she was not shy.

My 8th birthday was in July of this year. I had a party and a lot of friends and relatives came over. My gammie gave me a set of roller blades. She is so cool!

There is a new teacher at school this year. She is from India but talks like she was born here. She must be very smart. I learned a lot from her, especially about how different people are.

It was very cold this October. We even had snow before Halloween, which made trick-or-treating a little difficult. I should have dressed up as a snowplow.

1998

Writer's Jump Start

1 On a long strip of the adding-machine tape, make a time line of your life. Begin by printing the year you were born and label each year of your life, leaving about 12" (30 cm) of space after each year.

2 Look through the family albums and baby books for events to include. Ask your parents, grand-parents, siblings, and other family members, as well as other adults who know you well, for memories, funny stories, and other anecdotes that include you. Write them down on the scrap paper.

3 Choose the events to include on the time line and write them in sequence.

1 Begin at the beginning! On the writing paper, write about what your parents, brothers or sisters, or other adults told you about your first few weeks of life.

2 Think back to your first memories. Write small stories about what it was like to be little. Add details about what things seemed like to you back then. You probably saw everything as much larger than you do now! What did you like to do? What were you afraid of?

3 Review your time line and write about the "firsts" and other important events you included there. Bring these events to life by using interesting words and vivid descriptions.

4 Place all your stories in order. Copy them into your blank book or handmade book. Illustrate with sketches and photos if you like (please ask permission before using any photos from family photo albums).

Fabulous Firsts (and other fantastic family fun!)

Be sure not to leave important events like these out of your time line!

- ▶ births of brothers, sisters, and cousins

- ▶ trips and vacations

- ▶ the first day of school

- ▶ the first time you tried something like riding a bike or skiing

- ▶ a move to new house

- ▶ learning a hobby or skill: soccer camp, tennis lessons, a clay workshop

- ▶ making a special friend

- ▶ getting a new pet

- ▶ performances: school plays and concerts

- ▶ important family events: weddings, graduations, family reunions, and other memorable family gatherings

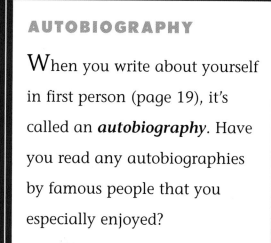

words for writers

AUTOBIOGRAPHY

When you write about yourself in first person (page 19), it's called an *autobiography*. Have you read any autobiographies by famous people that you especially enjoyed?

OUR FABULOUS FAMILY!

MAGAZINE

Boy Goes Hiking In Mountains

Girl Shows Incredible Green Thumb

Create your own family magazine full of stories, news, interviews, surveys, advice, word games, and more! Ask other family members to help with this project. If you like writing articles and combining them with photos to tell a story, see News Flash!, pages 63 to 66.

WHAT YOU NEED

Scrap paper

Pencil

Card stock

Markers or colored pencils

Computer and paper

Drawing paper

Scissors

Glue

Stapler

Strip of fabric or decorative tape

Writer's Jump Start

1 Make a list of what you want to include in your magazine. Assign articles to different family members. Include family vacations, neighborhood events, sports, or other topics of interest to your family. See WRITER'S JUMP START, page 64, for some article ideas.

2 Word games and puzzles are fun to include, too. How about an advice column or some letters to the editor? Have the artists in the family contribute cartoons and illustrations.

3 On the card stock, design and decorate a cover.

1 Write articles and review the ones written by other family members, making sure they include the "who, what, where, when, and why" of a good news story. Include photos, illustrations, or some fun cartoons (see CRAZY COMIC CAPERS, pages 115 to 117).

2 Create trivia games, crosswords, word searches, and other puzzles using family history and names.

3 Ask your family for anonymous advice questions. Then ask different family members to offer their advice as a response. Include them in a Dear Know-It-All column.

4 Collect and organize all the articles and other magazine pages. Type a table of contents. Stack the pages between the cover and staple the magazine together.

5 Glue fabric or put decorative tape over the staples. Watch as your magazine becomes a family favorite that's read over and over again!

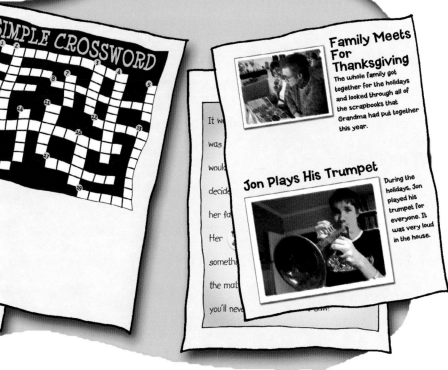

Ask Elsie

Dear Elsie,
My brother is always leaving his socks in the dining room, and the smell is ruining our dinners. Is there any way for me to help him understand how bad this is?
—Gasping in Poughkipsie

Dear Gasping,
What if all the family members who eat in the dining room sat down and had a conversation with your brother to explain the situation? Maybe then he would understand and find room for his stinky socks in the clothes hamper.
—Elsie

SIMPLE CROSSWORD

Family Meets For Thanksgiving

The whole family got together for the holidays and looked through all of the scrapbooks that Grandma had put together this year.

Jon Plays His Trumpet

During the holidays, Jon played his trumpet for everyone. It was very loud in the house.

Thanks for the Memories!

Every family has favorite stories that get told over and over again! Collect those one-of-a-kind family "folktales" (and maybe some tall tales!) that you want to be sure aren't forgotten. Practice your interviewing skills as you gather memories from family members large and small. Then preserve them in a unique collection!

WHAT YOU NEED

Notebook

Pencil

Writing paper

Extras: handmade book (see
THE WRITE STUFF, pages 5 to 6)

Writer's **Jump** Start

1 Decide on a theme for family stories you are interested in collecting. See page 109 for ideas.

2 Conduct interviews (see page 110 for tips). For those family members who don't live near you, gather information by phone or e-mail.

1 Look over the notes you gathered and decide which stories you want to write about.

2 Using the interview notes, write stories about each theme. They can be long or short, depending on your information. If you find that you're missing some details or that you forgot to ask a question or two, contact the person again with a few more questions.

3 Collect these stories in a handmade book or add them to scrapbooks and photo albums next to photos of those events.

Story Collections Might Include ...

Back when I was your age: Ask older relatives what it was like when they were kids. Find out what they played with, what their best friends were like, what kind of clothes they wore, and what they did for fun.

School days: It's fun to hear about what school was like for your parents, aunts, uncles, grandparents, and other older family members. Ask questions about their best and worst teachers, what they did at recess, and what their favorite subjects were. Did they ever get into trouble?

Holiday happenings: Collect stories about family members' favorite holiday celebrations. Even younger family members will have special memories to share.

Amazing adventures: Interview family members to learn their most amazing, scariest, or most surprising adventures.

Silly stories: Use interviews to help you find out about silly mix-ups and funniest family events.

Trips and travels: If your family likes to travel, how about a collection of vacation adventures?

Be an Interviewing Pro!

Write down a list of questions before the interview. The best interview questions get people talking. See how the questions on the left can be answered with one word, but the ones on the right will lead to some good stories?

Did you like school?	What was your favorite part of the school day and why?
Did you have a best friend?	Who were some of your special friends and how did you meet them?
Did you like bike riding?	Do you remember the first time you rode a two-wheeler? Tell me about it.

Write questions in a notebook, leaving several lines under each question to write responses.

Have another sheet available during the interview to write down information that doesn't fit under a question. You'll probably find that you'll think up new questions as you listen to your speaker. Write these questions on the separate sheet of paper as well as the answers.

Listen carefully and try not to interrupt. If the person gets totally off from the subject, however, go ahead and ask your next question.

Don't be shy about asking the person to slow down or to repeat if you missed writing something important.

THE FUNNY PAGES

Do you like telling jokes and funny stories that make people laugh? Maybe you know how to draw a crazy cat or a really silly-looking chicken. Find out how to create goofy characters, funny jokes, and silly, mixed-up stories. Turn your ideas into a comic book or a flip book, or mix your humor with others when you play Pass It On! No matter what project you create, it will be a success when you end up in stitches. So grab your clown-sized pencil or water-squirting pen and go for the giggles!

Make 'Em Laugh!

Think you can't write jokes? It's easier than you might imagine! If you like to laugh, then you can write funny jokes. Start with what makes *you* chuckle and turn it into humor that will make others laugh along with you!

Mom always said there were 3 kinds of people... Those who can count, and those who can't.

My Joke Book

WHAT YOU NEED

Notebook

Pencil

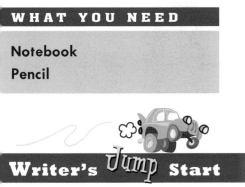

Writer's Jump Start

1 Use the notebook as a laugh log: Keep track of funny lines and situations in movies and books and on TV shows, as well as in real life, that make you laugh. Think about what makes something funny to you and your friends.

2 Many jokes use double meanings of words, called puns (at right), to be funny. Other jokes replace certain words with ones that sound similar:

> **Did the dolphin get you wet?**
> **Yes. He splashed me on porpoise.**

Sayings are also good joke material:

> **Why is the porcupine afraid?**
> **It is sitting on pins and needles.**

Keep your eyes and ears alert to how language is used in jokes. Write down funny jokes in your laugh log.

words for joke writers

a shutter-bug?

FUN WITH PUNS!

A *pun* is when you use a word in a funny way (sometimes changing it very slightly) to mean two different things. It's also called "a play on words." The READY TO WRITE section on page 114 is full of puns — can you find them all?

There is no sound in a vacuum. But the outside seems pretty noisy just the same.

1 Try starting a joke with a question. Use this formula: What did the _____ say to the _____? Fill in the blanks with different animals, people, or even objects. Then decide which answer could be changed slightly to lead to a double meaning. For example …

What did the turtle say to the frog? *I shell return.*

What did the cow say to the farmer? *Cud you leave me alone?*

What did the dog say to the squirrel? *Get off the woof.*

2 Try beginning jokes with other questions. See the examples below.

3 Write jokes as little stories — the more ridiculous, the better! Begin with a silly statement like: *A fish walked into a class-room.* Fish are usually in water, so this event takes readers by surprise and makes them want to read on. Write a few additional sentences before giving the *punch line* — the final, funny line that ends the joke. The whole joke might go like this:

A fish walked into a classroom. It took a seat beside me and took its school supplies out of its backpack. It turned and looked at me. "What are you staring at?" it asked. "Haven't you ever seen a fish in a school?"

Fish swim in schools, so the punch line is a pun (see page 113).

Why did the tree stay in the forest?

It couldn't leave.

What insect is a teacher's friend?

A spelling bee.

Why didn't the elephant get on the plane?

He forgot his trunk.

Crazy Comic Capers

Is the first section you turn to in the newspaper the comics? Me too!

Try creating your own comics and cartoons full of crazy characters! Before you know it,

you'll be filling entire comic books with their funny adventures.

WHAT YOU NEED

Scissors
Comics section from an old newspaper
Tape or glue
Drawing paper
Pencil

Writer's Jump Start

1 Practice cartoon drawing using newspaper comics. Cut out the bodies of your favorite comic-strip characters, attach them to a piece of paper, and draw on your own heads. Remember, exaggeration is key in cartooning!

2 Cut out some comic-character heads and create your own bodies to go with them.

3 Make some cartoons or comic strips showing your comic characters talking to cutouts of characters from the newspaper comics.

1 Now you're ready to try creating your own comic strip. Start simple: Draw one scene where one character is telling a joke to another. (See MAKE 'EM LAUGH! on page 112 for some ideas.)

2 Put different characters together and think of funny things they might say to each other. What would a cartoon mouse say to a cat? How about you and your younger brother, both as cartoon characters, talking to each other (see CARTOON SELF-PORTRAIT, page 117)? Try creating three to four scenes that show several related events. End with a punch line.

3 Develop more sophisticated cartoons by giving your characters personality. Exaggerate what they say just as you exaggerated their appearance. A character might like to brag, or be bossy or nervous. Well-rounded characters have strengths and weaknesses. It's funny to give a character an unlikely or unexpected trait. Maybe a big strong gorilla tries to hide from a small bossy mouse.

Russell Sprout

So birds should fly South for the fall and avoid the rush!

Ms. Grinder says you should stop talking to birds and come in because recess is over.

You tell Ms. Grinder that nothing short of an 800 lb. gorilla is going to make me come in before I want to!

4 How the characters relate to each other adds humor to the comic strip. One character might annoy another character by doing something over and over again, for example (think of *Peanuts* or *Garfield,* for example). Try developing ongoing relationships between some of your favorite cartoon characters.

Hello Ms. Grinder!

More Writer's Jump Starts

CARTOON SELF-PORTRAIT

Look into the back of a large metal spoon. Observe yourself from different angles. What big eyes you have! What a big nose! Make exaggerated faces, the sillier the better.

Draw the face you like the most on a big piece of paper and hang it it up. Cut out a large speech balloon and cover it with clear contact paper. Hang the balloon next to your portrait. Use an overhead transparency marker to write jokes and funny sayings. To change them, just wipe the words away and start over.

WORLD'S *Funniest* Flip Book

Use alliteration, action, and animation to create a flip book where the more you flip, the funnier it gets! What's the silliest situation you can come up with?

The huge hungry hippo

mixes macaroni

While playing soccer

An amazingly artistic alligator

mixes macaroni

While playing soccer

The risky red robot

creates a clay creature

While playing soccer

Drawing paper, 8½" x 11"
(21 x 27.5 cm), 3 sheets

Stapler

Pencil

Ruler

Scissors

Colored pencils

Writer's Jump Start

1 Fold the sheets of paper in half. Fit the pages together and staple together to make a book.

2 Draw two lines as shown. Cut along the lines through all pages.

3 Draw different animals in the three sections as shown. Make the drawings funny or silly by showing the animals doing human activities.

4 Flip the pages back and forth to make mixed-up animals. Adjust any lines to make the parts fit together. Color the drawings with colored pencils.

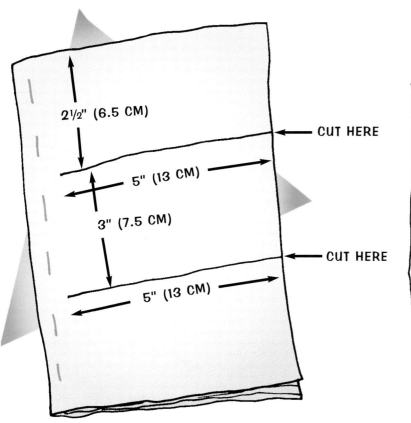

2½" (6.5 CM)

← CUT HERE

5" (13 CM)

3" (7.5 CM)

← CUT HERE

5" (13 CM)

In each top section, draw an animal head.

Draw an animal body in each of the middle sections.

Draw legs and feet in the bottom sections.

READY **2** WRITE

1 Write a description of each animal, using at least two **adjectives**. This flip book is a fun place to use *alliteration* (at right). Print these descriptions on the top section of each page. For example …

The goofy green gorilla

A fat friendly fish

A mangy musical monkey

The big bossy bear

2 In the middle sections, write descriptions of the actions pictured. Again use at least two descriptive words. For example …

paints pretty pictures

makes messy macaroni

blows big blue bubbles

3 In the bottom sections, write descriptions of the actions of each set of feet. Begin each line with "while." For example …

while roller-skating.

while hopping on one foot.

while doing the cancan.

words for writers

ALLITERATION

Alliteration means using words that all have the same beginning sound. You'll see it used in poetry, advertisements, newspaper headlines, and tongue twisters. After all, *five friendly frogs* is more fun to say than *several nice frogs,* don't you think?

Pass It On!

Creating this story is a group event. Play this writing game with family and friends. Take turns adding ideas and events and — suddenly! — you've got a crazy tale that is sure to get everyone laughing.

Two to four players
Pencils
Ruled index cards
Writing paper

Writer's Jump Start

Have all the players make up silly or funny situations that could happen in the middle of a story and write their ideas on the index cards. These will be the Suddenly Cards in the game. Keep the cards a secret from each other to add surprise. Suddenly Cards include situations such as …

You turn into an ice cube

You forget you are wearing pajamas

It starts to rain candy

You hear a plink-plink-plunk noise

A dog talks to you and asks for directions

1 Play begins with the first person writing three sentences to begin a story. He folds the paper to cover the first two lines of writing and passes the paper to the next writer.

2 The second writer adds on three more sentences, picking up from the last line. Again, the paper is folded over to reveal only the last line written before the story is passed to the next player.

3 Play continues until everyone has had a turn to add sentences.

4 The first player draws a Suddenly Card. She copies this sentence into the story and adds two more sentences of her own. The story is again folded so only the last line shows.

So there I was hanging from a tree by my toes. Suddenly my hair turned into lettuce.

5 As players take their turns, they have a choice of adding to the last line of the story or drawing a Suddenly Card.

6 Play ends when each player adds to the story three times. The first player writes the last line.

7 Read the finished story aloud to the group.

A

adjectives, 120. *See also* characters: traits
adventure stories, 7–26
  drawing cards, 24–26
  flip books, 21–23
  ideas for action/events, 8–9
  superheroes, 18–20 (*see also* tall tales)
  tiny explorers, 14–17
  treasure hunts, 6, 10–13
alliteration, 65, 120
animals, 9, 52–54, 78–80, 95–98
anthropomorphism, 117
assignment, reporter's, 64, 66
autobiographies/memoirs, 100–103. *See also* biographies; personal stories

B

biographies ("talking heads"), 56–59
books, handmade, 5–6. *See also* flip books; *and specific projects*
box, mystery in a, 44–47
brainstorming, 25

C

castle chronicles, 82–85
characters. *See also specific story types*
  comic/cartoon characters, 115–116
  development, 9 (*see also* plot)
  surprises involving, 98
  tiny characters, 14–17
  traits, 98, 116
cliff-hangers, 26
clues, 29, 30. *See also* mysteries
comics and cartoons, 115–117

D

defined terms. *See* writer's dictionary
detective stories. *See* mysteries
dialogue, 42, 43
dough recipe, 93

E

editing, 5, 66
explorers, stories about tiny, 14–17

F

fairy tales, 81, 92–98. *See also* fantasy; myths
family magazines, 104–106. *See also* newspapers

family story collections, 107–110
fantasy, 81–85, 92–98. *See also* fairy tales; myths; science fiction
first person point of view, 19
  adventure stories, 13
  autobiographies/memoirs, 100–103
  biographies ("talking heads"), 56–59
  science fiction and fairy tales, 68–70, 85, 87
  spy stories, 51
flip books, 21–23, 118–120
folktales and legends, 67–80
  legends from imaginary lands, 92–94
  magical-mask fables, 68–70
  myths, 78–80, 95–98
  tall tales, 71–74 (*see also* superhero stories)
  trickster stories, 75–77

G

group writing projects, 62, 63–66, 104–106, 121–123

H

haunted house stories, 37–39
headlines, 65
"How I Met My Robot Friend" (Nick), 6

how-to books, 60–62
humor, 111–123
  comics and cartoons, 115–117
  flip books, 118–120
  jokes and puns, 112–114
  pass-it-on stories, 121–123

I

illustrations, 6. *See also* maps; photographs; rebuses; *and specific projects*
imaginary lands, 92–94. *See also* maps
interviews, 107–110

J

jigsaw puzzles, 31–33
jokes, 112–114
journalism, 63–66. *See also* family magazines

L

layout, 65–66
lead, 65, 66
legends. *See* folktales and legends

M

magazines, family, 104–106
magic, 85. *See also* fairy tales; fantasy; myths; superhero stories

maps, 10–13. *See also* imaginary lands

masks, fables about magical, 68–70

monologues, 59. *See also* biographies

mysteries, 6, 27–54
    clues, 29
    haunted house stories, 37–39
    ideas for action/events, 28
    mystery in a box, 44–47
    pet mysteries, 6, 52–54
    spooky sounds stories, 34–36
    spy stories, 48–51
    triple puzzlers, 31–33
    writer's dictionary, 30, 51

myths, 78–80, 95–98

N

newspapers, 63–66. *See also* comics and cartoons; family magazines

nonfiction writing, 55–66
    autobiographies/memoirs, 100–103
    biographies ("talking heads"), 56–59
    family magazines, 104–106
    family story collections, 107–110
    how-to books, 60–62
    newspapers, 63–66

O

organization
    fictional plots (*see* plot organization/planning)
    how-to books, 61

P

papier-mâché recipe, 57

pass-it-on stories, 121–123

personal stories, 99–110. *See also* biographies
    autobiographies/memoirs, 100–103
    cartoon self-portrait, 117
    family magazines, 104–106
    family story collections, 107–110

pets
    newspaper section, 64
    pet mysteries, 6, 52–54

photographs, 53, 57, 65

plays, 40–43

plot organization/planning, 9. *See also specific story types*
    drawing cards, 24–26
    mapping, 10–13, 15–16
    sound effects, 36

point of view, 19
    first person point of view, 13, 19, 51, 56–59, 68–70, 85, 87, 100–103

tiny explorer characters, 15–16

power of three, 97

presentation, 5–6. *See also specific projects*

props, 41, 43

puns, 113–114

R

reading suggestions, 72, 75

rebuses, 31–33

red herrings, 30, 47

research, 57

robot stories, 6, 89–91

S

salt dough recipe, 93

science fiction, 6, 81, 86–91. *See also* fairy tales; fantasy; superhero stories

scripts, 41–43

second person point of view, 19

setting, creating the. *See* imaginary lands; maps; *and specific story types*

similes, 73–74

sound effects, 34–36

space-travel tales, 86–88. *See also* science fiction

spooky sounds stories, 6, 34–36

spy stories, 48–51

superhero stories, 18–20. *See also* masks; tall tales

suspense, 8, 51. *See also* mysteries

T

"talking heads," 56–59

tall tales, 71–74. *See also* folktales and legends

text, presentation of, 6. *See also specific projects*

third person point of view, 19

three, power of, 97

tiny explorer stories, 14–17

treasure hunt stories, 6, 10–13

trickster stories, 75–77

true stories. *See* nonfiction writing

V

verbs, 91

voice. *See* point of view

W

writer's dictionary
    mystery-writing terms, 30
    news-reporting (journalism) terms, 66
    play-writing terms, 43
    spy story-writing terms, 51

More Award-winning Books from Williamson

Welcome to Williamson Books! Our books are available from your bookseller or directly from Williamson Books at Ideals Publications. Please see the next page for ordering information or to visit our website. Thank you.

All books are suitable for children ages 7 through 14 and older, and are 120 to 128 pages, 11 x 8 ½, $12.95, unless otherwise noted.

In full color!
WORDPLAY CAFÉ
Cool Codes, Priceless Punzles®
& Phantastic Phonetic Phun
*written and illustrated
by Michael Kline*

GREAT GAMES!
Old & New, Indoor/Outdoor, Travel,
Board, Ball & Word
by Sam Taggar

PARENTS' CHOICE RECOMMENDED
FOREWORD MAGAZINE
BOOK OF THE YEAR FINALIST
PAPER-FOLDING FUN!
50 Awesome Crafts to Weave,
Twist & Curl
by Ginger Johnson

In full color!
USING COLOR IN YOUR ART!
Choosing Colors for Impact
& Pizzazz
by Sandi Henry

Over 100,000 sold!
KIDS COOK!
Fabulous Food for the Whole Family
*by Sarah Williamson and
Zachary Williamson*

PARENTS' CHOICE APPROVED
PARENT'S GUIDE CHILDREN'S MEDIA AWARD
BOREDOM BUSTERS!
The Curious Kids' Activity Book
by Avery Hart and Paul Mantell

PARENTS' CHOICE APPROVED
DR. TOY BEST VACATION PRODUCT
KIDS GARDEN!
The Anytime, Anyplace Guide to
Sowing & Growing Fun
by Avery Hart and Paul Mantell

AMERICAN BOOKSELLER PICK OF THE LISTS
OPPENHEIM TOY PORTFOLIO BEST BOOK AWARD
PARENTS' CHOICE APPROVED
SUMMER FUN!
60 Activities for a
Kid-Perfect Summer
by Susan Williamson

PARENTS' CHOICE RECOMMENDED
ORBUS PICTUS AWARD
FOR OUTSTANDING NONFICTION
KIDS' ART WORKS!
Creating with Color, Design,
Texture & More
by Sandi Henry

TEACHERS' CHOICE AWARD
DR. TOY BEST VACATION PRODUCT
CUT-PAPER PLAY!
Dazzling Creations from Construction Paper
by Sandi Henry

PARENTS' CHOICE APPROVED AWARD
THE KIDS'
MULTICULTURAL CRAFT BOOK
35 Crafts from Around the World
by Roberta Gould

PARENTS' CHOICE GOLD AWARD
AMERICAN BOOKSELLER PICK OF THE LISTS
THE KIDS'
MULTICULTURAL ART BOOK
Art & Craft Experiences from
Around the World
by Alexandra Michaels Terzian

THE KIDS' BOOK OF
INCREDIBLY FUN CRAFTS
by Roberta Gould

PARENTS' CHOICE RECOMMENDED
THE KIDS' GUIDE TO
MAKING SCRAPBOOKS
& PHOTO ALBUMS!
How to Collect, Design, Assemble, Decorate
by Laura Check

PARENTS' CHOICE RECOMMENDED
KIDS' EASY-TO-CREATE
WILDLIFE HABITATS
for Small Spaces in City, Suburbs
& Countryside
by Emily Stetson

IN THE DAYS OF DINOSAURS
A Rhyming Romp through Dino History
by Howard Temperley
64 pages, 11 x 8 ½, full color, all ages, $9.95

PARENTS' CHOICE GOLD AWARD
BENJAMIN FRANKLIN
BEST JUVENILE NONFICTION AWARD
KIDS MAKE MUSIC!
Clapping & Tapping from Bach to Rock!
by Avery Hart and Paul Mantell

HANDS AROUND THE WORLD
365 Creative Ways to Build
Cultural Awareness & Global Respect
by Susan Milord

In full color!
THE MYSTERIOUS
SECRET LIFE OF MATH
Uncover How (& Why) Numbers Survived
from the Cave Dwellers to Us
by Ann McCallum

PARENTS' CHOICE RECOMMENDED
CHILDREN'S DIGEST HEALTH EDUCATION AWARD
THE KIDS' GUIDE TO
FIRST AID
All about Bruises, Burns, Stings, Sprains
& Other Ouches
by Karen Buhler Gale, R.N.

PARENTS' CHOICE APPROVED
BENJAMIN FRANKLIN
BEST MULTICULTURAL BOOK AWARD
THE KIDS'
MULTICULTURAL COOKBOOK
Food & Fun Around the World
by Deanna F. Cook

PARENTS' CHOICE HONOR AWARD
SKIPPING STONES
ECOLOGY & NATURE AWARD
MONARCH MAGIC!
Butterfly Activities & Nature Discoveries
by Lynn M. Rosenblatt
96 pages, 8 x 10, 100 full-color photos

PARENTS' CHOICE RECOMMENDED
THE KIDS' BOOK OF
WEATHER FORECASTING
Build a Weather Station,
"Read" the Sky & Make Predictions!
*with meteorologist Mark Breen
& Kathleen Friestad*

PARENTS' CHOICE HONOR AWARD
AMERICAN INSTITUTE OF PHYSICS
SCIENCE WRITING AWARD
GIZMOS & GADGETS
Creating Science Contraptions that Work
(& Knowing Why)
by Jill Frankel Hauser

AMERICAN BOOKSELLER PICK OF THE LISTS
PARENTS' CHOICE RECOMMENDED
ADVENTURES IN ART
Arts & Crafts Experiences
for 8- to 13-Year-Olds
by Susan Milord

The following *Quick Starts for Kids!*® books are 64 pages, 8 ½ x 11, for everyone ages 8 to 88, fully illustrated, $8.95.

MAKE YOUR OWN BIRDHOUSES & FEEDERS

CREATE YOUR OWN CANDLES
30 Easy-to-Make Designs

GARDEN FUN!
Indoors & Out;
In Pots & Small Spots

MAKE YOUR OWN COOL CARDS
25 Awesome Notes & Invitations!

DRAWING HORSES
(that look *real!*)

DRAW YOUR OWN CARTOONS!

BE A CLOWN!
Techniques from a Real Clown

YO-YO!
Tips & Tricks from a Pro

KIDS' EASY KNITTING PROJECTS

In full color!
KNITTING II
More Easy-to-Make Knitting Projects

In full color!
PUPPETS AND PUPPET THEATERS

BAKE THE BEST-EVER COOKIES!

KIDS' EASY QUILTING PROJECTS

KIDS' EASY BIKE CARE
Tune-Ups, Tools & Quick Fixes

40 KNOTS TO KNOW
Hitches, Loops, Bends & Bindings

ALMOST-INSTANT SCRAPBOOKS

REALLY COOL FELT CRAFTS

MAKE YOUR OWN FUN FRAMES!

MAKE YOUR OWN HAIRWEAR
Beaded Barrettes, Clips,
Dangles & Headbands

MAKE YOUR OWN CHRISTMAS ORNAMENTS

MAKE YOUR OWN TEDDY BEARS & BEAR CLOTHES

3 Easy Ways to Order Books:

Please visit our secure website to place your order.

Toll-free phone orders: 1-800-586-2572

Toll-free fax orders: 1-888-815-2759

All major credit cards accepted
(please include the number and expiration date).

Or, send a check with your order to:

Williamson Books, Orders
535 Metroplex Drive, Suite 250
Nashville, TN 37211

Please add $4.00 for postage for one book plus $1.00 for each additional book. Satisfaction is guaranteed or full refund without questions or quibbles.